OLIVER TWIST

A Play for Young Audiences

Based on the Novel by Charles Dickens
Adapted by Muriel Browne

Acting Edition

Classic Youth Plays
Theatre Arts Press

NOTE: This play may be performed without a royalty, however the making of copies from this book is strictly prohibited.

For more information on producing this play and for a list of titles published, visit:

ClassicYouthPlays.com

Printed in the United States of America

9 8 7 6 5 4 3 2

Muriel Browne was a children's theatre visionary and was instrumental in establishing the children's theatre at the Goodman Theatre School of Drama where she was one of its first directors. She studied theatre at Carnegie Institute and on her return to Chicago she became involved in Chicago's Theatre of Youth Federal Theatre Project where she directed many plays including her own play *Teller of Tales*. She was the first director of the children's theatre department of the Goodman Theatre where she sought to bring the classics to younger audiences. Her adaptation of *Oliver Twist* was first performed at the Goodman.

Cast of Characters

Fagin

Oliver Twist

Nancy

Dodger

Monks

Bill Sykes

Mrs. Bedwin

Brownlow

Grimwig

Mr. Bumble

Mrs. Bumble

Harry Maylie

Rose

Mrs. Maylie

ACT ONE

Scene 1
A Room in Fagin's Quarters

Scene 2
The Parlor of Mr. Brownlow's House

Scene 3
Fagin's Quarters

ACT TWO

Scene 1
Fagin's Quarters, the Next Morning

Scene 2
Brownlow's House, Several Months Later

ACT ONE

Scene 1

A room in Fagin's quarters, which is the meeting-place for a group of thieves. The walls and ceiling are black with age and dirt, and spiders and rats inhabit the corners of the room. There is a table, on which are dirty plates, broken bottles with candles stuck into them, and a few old spoons and forks, and one long knife. Rough stools, broken chairs, and kegs make up the other furniture.

On a rough pallet, a boy is sleeping. The only other occupant of the room is a dirty-shriveled-up old man. He is villainous and repulsive-looking, with matted red hair, and long, thin fingers that, look like claws. Everything about him gives the impression of age and evil. He is FAGIN. He goes to the sleeping boy, looks down on him, touches him with his foot to make sure he is asleep, then goes to a great pile of dirty rags and old clothes which take up a entire corner of the room. He glances back at the boy, then kneels and pulls out from under the rags an old, battered, red leather box. He takes it to the table, and still keeping a watchful eye on the boy, he sits and opens the box, taking out several watches and chains. He fingers them lovingly, and. talks aloud to them. In his greed, he forgets to watch the boy, and during his speech, OLIVER opens his eyes, and raises himself on one elbow to watch the curious scene. He is a fair-haired boy of twelve, with a frank, open face and an engaging smile. He, too, is poorly dressed, but cleaner and more respectable-looking than FAGIN.

FAGIN. *(Fondling the watches.)* Aha! Clever dogs! Clever dogs, every one of 'em…and staunch to the last man. Never even told the parson where the loot was hidden. Never peached on old Fagin. Fine fellows…fine fellows, and all of 'em strung up in a row — all five of 'em. But they never peached on old Fagin…they never betrayed their old teacher. *(He singles out one watch.)* Aha! There's a pretty watch now…and a darlin' thing it is to own, too. *(He looks up suddenly.)* What's that? *(He remembers the boy, and turns quickly to look at. him.)* Why do you watch me? Why are you awake? *(He rises and goes toward OLIVER with the long knife.)* What have you seen? Quick, boy, speak! For your life, speak!

OLIVER. I didn't mean to disturb you, sir, but I couldn't sleep any longer.

FAGIN. *(Grasping him.)* How long have you been awake?

OLIVER. Only for a minute, sir.

FAGIN. Are you sure? Don't lie to me, boy.

OLIVER. Oh, yes, quite sure.

FAGIN. *(Releasing him, then suddenly swinging on him again.)* Did you see the watches?

OLIVER. Yes, sir, I saw them.

FAGIN. They're mine. My little property, and all I have to live on in my old age, Oliver.

OLIVER. But you have so many. Where did you get them all?

FAGIN. I collect them. It's a little hobby of mine. Folks call me a miser, my dear, but it's a harmless little diversion, collecting watches.

(He puts them back into the box.)

OLIVER. May I get up now?

FAGIN. By all means, get up You've slept half the morning now. *(He indicates a broken pitcher near the fire.)* There's a pitcher of water, and on the keg yonder is a basin to wash yourself in. Not such fine accommodations as you've been accustomed to, perhaps, but the best I have, Oliver. The best I have.

OLIVER. *(Pouring the water into the basin.)* I've not been used to fine accommodations, sir — not where I've been. We didn't even have a basin, and most of the time there wasn't any fire — except in the kitchen.

(When OLIVER'S back is turned, FAGIN slips the box under the rags again, and pulls out a dirty-looking towel.)

FAGIN. Here's a towel for you. *(He losses it to OLIVER, then goes up to the fire.)* Now we'll soon have breakfast and you must tell me more about yourself.

(He begins to make preparations for the breakfast.)

OLIVER. There isn't much to tell.

FAGIN. But you haven't told us anything yet. We don't even know where you came from.

OLIVER. I came from the country. I told you that, sir.

FAGIN. Aye, but your folks, lad. What about your folks?

OLIVER. *(As he scrubs his neck.)* I haven't any.

FAGIN. Don't wash so hard. It isn't good for boys to be too clean. Not in such cold weather. Where did you stay before the Dodger found you and brought you here last night?

OLIVER. Just anywhere. Why do you call him the Dodger?

FAGIN. The Artful Dodger, we calls him. It's a nickname we give him because he can work his way in and out, and nobody knows he's there, until he's gone. How did you get to London?

OLIVER. I walked. I walked for seven days, and I was so tired and hungry when the Dodger found me —

FAGIN. Beak's orders' eh?

OLIVER. Beaks? I don't understand. Is that a kind of a bird?

FAGIN. My eye, how green you are! A beak is a magistrate, and when a magistrate says walk — you walk.

OLIVER. Oh no, it wasn't a magistrate, sir.

FAGIN. *(Hearing a sound.)* What's that?

OLIVER. I didn't hear a thing, sir.

FAGIN. *(Goes to the door right, and listens.)* Someone's down there. I must train your ears, boy. *(A bell rings.)* There's the tinkler…and there are two of 'em. I heard two steps. *(He unbolts the door, and opens it a crack, calling through it.)* Who's down there?

DODGER. *(Off.)* The Dodger.

FAGIN. What do you say?

DODGER. Plummy and slam.

FAGIN. Who's with you?

DODGER. Only Nancy.

FAGIN. Come up, then. *(He closes the door, and addresses OLIVER.)* Well, did you hear that?

OLIVER. I couldn't hear what he said.

FAGIN. Sometimes I have to go out, and then you'll be here alone. And if that bell rings, never let 'em in until you know who they are. And if they don't give the word, lock up and don't let 'em in.

OLIVER. What is the word, sir?

FAGIN. If you heard what the Dodger said, you'd know. "Plummy and slam," he said, and all my friends knows it. And they always gives it when they come. It's a darlin' thing to have friends, Oliver — friends you can depend on, I mean. *(Knock at the door. FAGIN opens it again.)* Come in, Nancy, my dear. We're always glad to see you. Well, Dodger, did you bring your appetite with you? Ready for breakfast, both of you?

(NANCY is a pretty, hard-faced young woman in cheap, gaudy clothes. She looks at OLIVER critically as she enters. The DODGER, while very little older than OLIVER, is already a man of experience, and does credit to FAGIN'S teaching. He is swaggering and bold, with a sly manner when he wants to assume it. His clothes are too large for him, and his hat is stuck on top of his head at such an angle, that it seems about to fall off. His coat sleeves are turned back on his arms to get his hands out, and his coat is much too long for him. He speaks in a loud, insolent tone.)

DODGER. Hallo, my covey.

NANCY. Hallo, Fagin. Who's the young 'un, Dodger?

(FAGIN relocks the door and goes on with breakfast preparations.)

DODGER. That's him — the one I told you about. Peaked, ain't he.

NANCY. Hallo.

OLIVER. Good morning, Miss…?

NANCY. Just Nancy. What's yours?

OLIVER. Oliver. Oliver Twist.

NANCY. Is that really your name — Twist?

OLIVER. I never had any other. It's the name they gave me when I was born.

NANCY. *(Laughing.)* Twist! Twist! Lord, lord, what a name!

DODGER. *(Laughing too.)* I never thought of it — but it is funny, ain't it?

FAGIN. Now, now, don't plague the boy. Any luck this morning, Dodger? I hope you have been hard at work.

DODGER. Hard as nails.

FAGIN. Good boy! What have you got?

DODGER. *(Producing them.)* A couple of pocketbooks.

FAGIN. *(As he takes them.)* Well lined?

DODGER. I've done better.

FAGIN. Not as heavy as they might be. *(Examining the workmanship.)* But very neat and nicely made, ain't they, Oliver? Good workman, ain't he?

OLIVER. Yes, sir, they are very neatly made.

NANCY. Lord save us! He's so green, you wouldn't know him from grass in the country.

FAGIN. Anything else?

DODGER. A couple of wipes.

(*He gives FAGIN two large handkerchiefs.*)

FAGIN. Not so bad. Not so bad. That's a darlin' one. (*He looks for the marks in the corners.*) And now we'll have to teach Oliver to do the marks. Would you like to do the marks, Oliver?

OLIVER. But they are already marked, sir.

(*They all laugh at him again.*)

FAGIN. So they are, but not the way we want them. So we pick them out carefully with a needle, and then we wash them — and sell them.

DODGER. You're right, Nancy. He's so jolly green, I'll die laughing at him.

NANCY. But he's a good young 'un. To think we was like that once.

DODGER. I never was.

NANCY. No, you was born a —

FAGIN. (*Breaking in.*) Hold your tongue, Nancy. Take those sausages off the fire, Dodger. Bring up the old keg. Oliver. You can sit on that. (*They do as he tells them.*) Now, my dears, while you have breakfast, I'll tidy up. (*Draws NANCY aside.*) See if you can draw him out a bit. He is so close-mouthed, he won't say a word.

NANCY. All the better for our business, I'm thinkin'.

FAGIN. That's so, too. But it's just as well for us to know somethin' about him. There's somethin' he hasn't told us yet, and when we knows that, we can hold him here.

NANCY. I'll try, but it does seem a pity. Such a nice kid like him —

FAGIN. It ain't like you to be soft, Nancy.

NANCY. I know, but —

FAGIN. But that's all. I told you a long time ago there wasn't any place for sentiment in our business, Nancy.

(*He starts to cross away and as he passes the DODGER, DODGER trips him and sends him sprawling to the floor.*)

NANCY. (*As she helps FAGIN to rise.*) Dodger!

FAGIN. You limb of Satan! I'll teach you to try your tricks on me!

DODGER. (*Laughs.*) Didn't you teach me to trip honest folks and make 'em fall?

FAGIN. If I did, you needn't trip me.

> (*He starts toward the DODGER, who holds up the pan of sausages in his hand threatening.*)

DODGER. No, no, you ain't honest. Let me alone, or I'll throw hot grease on you.

NANCY. Go along now, and don't mind his monkey tricks. Here, give me them sausages. You don't have to make the floor any dirtier — *(Takes pan away from DODGER.)* Now sit down there and eat your breakfast.

FAGIN. *(Still grumbling.)* Ungrateful dog, that's, what he is! Tripping me up! After all I've done for you. Where would you be, without me, I'd like to know?

DODGER. In jail, no doubt.

FAGIN. And it's in jail you'll be yet, if you don't watch out.

DODGER. Ain't I the Dodger? It'll be a sharp Beak what tells me to walk.

NANCY. *(Urging FAGIN through the door.)* Go along now, and let us eat.

> (*She pushes FAGIN into the next room, but he speaks over her shoulder before she can close the door.*)

FAGIN. Yes, you're riding high now, and you can talk with the best of 'em. But don't forget it was old Fagin that put you there.

> (*NANCY pushes him in and closes the door.*)

DODGER. (Calling after him.) I ain't likely to forget it, with you remindin' me all the time.

NANCY. *(Slaps him as she passes.)* Hold your tongue now, Dodger, and let's eat in peace. *(Breaks off bread from loaf.)* Why, you ain't give Oliver a bite to eat.

> (*She sits at the table.*)

DODGER. *(With his month full.)* He's got two hands, ain't he?

NANCY. You must be starved. Here.

OLIVER. I'm not so hungry as when I came last night.

DODGER. You should a-seen him then. He eat like a starved wolf.

NANCY. *(Giving him sausages.)* Where's your home, Oliver?

OLIVER. I haven't any home.

NANCY. But you must have had one once.

OLIVER. No, I never had any home.

NANCY. Where did you stay?

OLIVER. In the Workhouse. I was born there.

NANCY. And your mother and father — was they there too?

OLIVER. My mother was — for one night. She died when I was born. An old woman there told me about her — Mrs. Thingummy — but she's dead, too.

DODGER. *(Lauhging with his mouth full.)* Thingummmm —

NANCY. Hold your din. And your father?

OLIVER. I don't know anything about him. I don't know his name, even.

NANCY. Then your name ain't Twist?

OLIVER. No, but that's the name they gave me. They named us by the alphabet. The last one before me was an S, so I was a T.

NANCY. Yes, but why Twist?

OLIVER. I don't know. My, but these sausages are good. We hardly ever had meat — just gruel. And once, when I asked for more, they beat me.

NANCY. *(putting more sausages on his plate.)* Here, have some more sausages.

DODGER. *(Reaches for the pan.)* Whose sausages are those?

NANCY. Sit down. Dodger. Did you run away from the Workhouse because you was hungry?

OLIVER. No, from the undertaker's.

NANCY. The undertaker's?

OLIVER. Yes. Mr. Sowerberry. I was apprenticed to him. I slept with the coffins.

DODGER. That must have been pleasant. See any ghosts?

OLIVER. Oh no, it wasn't so bad after you got used to it. And I went to all the funerals. And sometimes the people would give me a penny. Mr. Sowerberry wasn't so bad, but Mrs. Sowerberry was.

NANCY. And then you came to London.

OLIVER. Yes, I walked, and I was so cold and hungry when the Dodger found me, I thought I was going to die, but he brought me here, and Mr. Fagin has been very good to me.

DODGER. The old fox will be good to you just as long as you do what he says, and don't talk to nobody outside.

OLIVER. He must be rich, to have so many watches.

DODGER. *(Suddenly interested.)* Watches!

OLIVER. Oh yes, a whole box full of them. I saw them this morning

DODGER. Where does he keep them, Oliver?

NANCY. Dodger! You wouldn't!

DODGER. Couldn't I? Say, where does he keep them?

OLIVER. I — I didn't see him put them away.

NANCY. Ask Fagin yourself if you want to know. Don't try to put it on the boy.

DODGER. I don't dare ask him. You know his temper.

NANCY. It ain't as bad as Bill's, though.

DODGER. I guess nobody's temper is as bad as Bill Sykes'. Sometimes he's so mean, even his dog hates him.

OLIVER. Does — does he ever come here?

DODGER. Sure, he's one of us. He'll be along after a while.

NANCY. He's been gone for a few days — on business for Fagin. But he ought to be back today.

DODGER. And remember, don't answer him back. Nobody ever answers Bill back. And if he tells you to do something, why you do it, and do it quick. *(The bell rings again.)* There's the tinkler. Maybe that's Bill. *(Goes to door, opens it a little, and calls out.)* Who's there?

MONKS. *(Off.)* It's Monks.

DODGER. What do you say?

MONKS. Plummy and slam.

DODGER. All right. Come up.

> *(He closes the door.)*

NANCY. *(Eagerly.)* Was it Bill?

FAGIN. *(Entering from left.)* Who is it?

DODGER. It's your precious friend Monks.

FAGIN. Ah, Monks, is it? Pick up things a little, Nancy. It's been some time since he honored us with a visit.

NANCY. *(Throwing a few things into the cornert.)* He's a rum one. I don't like him.

FAGIN. *(Opening the door.)* Come in, Monks. Come in.

(MONKS enters. He is a tall not. bad-looking man in his late twenties. He is not so poorly dressed as the others, but not so far removed from them as to seem well-dressed. He is more like a man wearing a too perfect disguise. He speaks their lingo, but there is evidence of education, and not altogether lost refinement about him. A red scar shows on his throat, above his neckerchief.)

MONKS. Can't you get those stairs fixed? Some day I'll break a leg down there, and then you'll answer for it. Hello, Dodger.

FAGIN. *(Closes the door.)* It's been so long since you was here, Monks, you've forgotten the old stairs. We know every broken corner, don't we, Nancy?

NANCY. Hallo.

MONKS. *(Grunts and looks at OLIVER.)* Who's the boy?

FAGIN. One of Fagin's boys. A new one. Oliver Twist.

MONKS. Twist?

FAGIN. Oliver, this is Monks, a good friend of ours, and always welcome, though he don't come often.

OLIVER. How do you do, sir.

FAGIN. Nice manners, ain't he?

MONKS. Twist...

NANCY. Go on! It's just a made-up name they gave him in the Workhouse.

MONKS. *(Seizing OLIVER by the shoulders, and looking into his face.)* In the Workhouse?

OLIVER. Yes. I was born in the Workhouse, and my mother died there. I never had a real name.

MONKS. Where is this Workhouse? Come, don't be afraid to tell me. I won't peach on you if you've run away.

OLIVER. In the country.

MONKS. *(Laughing ironically to himself.)* It's a rum go! In fact, it's perfect! And what luck that you should fall in with old Fagin!

OLIVER. Yes, sir.

MONKS. Who is in charge there now?

OLIVER. Mr. and Mrs. Bumble, sir.

MONKS. *(Scribbling on his cuff.)* Bumble.

OLIVER. Oh sir, you're not going to send me back, are you? You promised, you know.

MONKS. Don't worry. I'll never send you back there. I just want to — to make some inquiries about the place.

OLIVER. Can I tell you anything, sir?

MONKS. No, you wouldn't know. It was a long time ago. About the time you were born.

> *(Grunt from the DODGER. FAGIN silences him.)*

FAGIN. Have some sausages, Monks?

MONKS. *(After looking them over.)* No. Are you going out again, Dodger?

DODGER. I might.

MONKS. You, Nancy?

NANCY. No, I'm waitin' for Bill. He ought to be back this mornin'.

MONKS. Run along, the lot of you. I want to talk to Fagin — in private.

DODGER. Huh! Come on, Nancy. I guess he means us.

MONKS. How about the boy?

FAGIN. He ain't ready to go out yet.

DODGER. Ah, let him come along. I'll look after him.

FAGIN. No, he can't go out yet.

MONKS. Let him go, Fagin. The Dodger can look after him.

> *(MONKS takes FAGIN aside and talks to him.)*

OLIVER. Are you going back to your work, Dodger?

DODGER. Sure, too bad you ain't a prig too.

NANCY. He doesn't know what a prig is.

OLIVER. I think I do — now. You're one, aren't you?

DODGER. Sure I am. And so's Fagin — and Monks — and Nancy and Bill Sykes. And Bill's dog, too. He's a rum one. Why, he wouldn't even bark in a witness box, for fear of committin' himself. Sure, we're all prigs, we are, and we stand by each other, too. And we don't give each other away. You're one of us now, and you can't peach on us — see?

NANCY.   He means you can't tell on us. No thief ever gives another one away. That is, no real thief ever does.

DODGER.   You're right they don't. And if any sneakin', white-livered rat ever does try it, we get him, and it's the last time he ever peaches. Don't you forget that.

MONKS. That's not an idle threat, boy. You understand?

OLIVER.   Yes, sir. I understand.

MONKS.   All right. And don't you forget it.

FAGIN.   Well, take him along, Dodger, but mind you keep an eye on him, and don't let him talk to anyone.

DODGER.   All right, old bag of bones. Get your cap, Oliver. Come along, Nancy. It's the cold, cold world for us. *(Goes to door.)* Don't worry, Fagin. I'll cut his eye teeth for him.

FAGIN.   Now mind you don't try anything with him. Just you walk around and mind your own business, and bring him back here in a few minutes.

DODGER.   All right. All right.

(They go out, and FAGIN closes and locks the door after them.)

FAGIN.   Now, Monks, what is it?

MONKS.   It's that boy.

FAGIN.   Well, what about him

MONKS.   I'll find those Workhouse people and make sure.

FAGIN.   That boy ain't done nothing. Why, he's so innocent it's funny. That's why he's so valuable. Does he look like one of us? No one would ever suspect him, to look at him.

MONKS.   That boy is somebody. And if he's the boy I think he is, I'll pay you to make him a criminal. I want him to be a thief, Fagin, and a bold one. And then I want him to be caught and sent to prison.

FAGIN.   What are you drivin' at? You never set eyes on him before today.

MONKS.   I know what I'm about, and I want him out of the way. Just teach him all your tricks, Fagin, and leave it to him to be caught.

FAGIN.   You'll pay me to do it, you say? How much?

MONKS. I'll settle that when I've seen these Workhouse people, but I'll make it worth your while.

FAGIN. All right, Monks. Now what did you come to see me about?

MONKS. I told you. The boy.

FAGIN. You didn't come here to talk about that boy. You'd never seen him before, and you didn't know he was here.

MONKS. Well, I've seen him now. I'll write to the Workhouse this week, and get those Bumbles up to London. There's someone at the door.

FAGIN. *(Hurries to the door.).* I didn't hear the tinkler. *(Speaks through the door.)* Who's there?

NANCY. *(Outside.)* It's me — Nancy.

FAGIN. *(As he opens the door.)* It's only Nancy. What is it, my dear?

NANCY. I forgot my shawl.

MONKS. *(Crossing to the door.)* The devil! You can't trust any of them.

FAGIN. Come again. Monks. You're always welcome.

MONKS. I'll come when there ain't so many around.

NANCY. I was here first.

> *(MONKS goes out, and FAGIN locks the door.)*

FAGIN. How did you get in? I didn't hear the bell.

NANCY. I didn't go out. I came back for my shawl.

FAGIN. It didn't take you all that time to come up the steps. Monks was right. You was listenin'.

NANCY. *(As he comes toward her.)* Don't you put your hands on me, or I'll tell Bill. Why should I want to listen at the door?

FAGIN. You think a lot of Bill, don't you?

NANCY. When he's good to me, I do. But sometimes when he's —

FAGIN. Don't say it. Nancy. When you're as old as I am, you'll learn to keep still.

NANCY. And when I'm that old, Bill won't want me any more, and then what will I do?

FAGIN. You won't be old for a long time, my dear. Not for a long time. *(Catches her arm.)* Now then — did you listen, or not?

NANCY. Let me go. You're hurting me.

FAGIN. Tell me. Did you listen?

NANCY. Yes, I did listen.

FAGIN. I never knew you to do that before.

NANCY. I don't trust that Monks. He's too slick.

FAGIN. He's all right. He's one of us.

NANCY. He wasn't always one of us. He's different, and smarter.

FAGIN. He isn't smart enough to fool old Fagin. None of 'em are smart enough for that.

(*Bell is heard.*)

NANCY. That'll be Bill.

FAGIN. (*At the door.*) Who's there?

BILL. (*Off.*) Bill.

FAGIN. What do you say?

BILL. Plummy and slam.

FAGIN. All right. Come up. Bill. (*To NANCY.*) We won't tell Bill, will we? Just a little misunderstandin' between ourselves.

NANCY. No, I won't tell Bill. (*BILL enters.*) Hallo, Bill.

(*BILL SYKES is a. big stoutly-built fellow. His face is heavy and hard, and his eyes are small and cruel. He is roughly dressed. He is a bully, and they all know it, but he is not afraid to tackle anything in his line, including house-breaking.*)

BILL. What are you up to now, you greasy old fence? What's he been saying to you, Nancy?

NANCY. Nothing, Bill.

FAGIN. Good morning, Mr. Skyes.

BILL. Well, just you tell me if he ever tries any tricks with you. (*To FAGIN.*) You can ill treat your boys, but you can't touch her. (*NANCY takes his scarf.*) I wonder they don't do you in. I'd have done it long ago if I'd been your prentice, but I couldn't 'a sold you afterward, for you're fit for nothing but keeping as a curiosity of ugliness. And I reckon they don't blow glass bottles big enough to put you in.

FAGIN. (*As he locks the door.*) Not so loud, Mr. Sykes. Not so loud.

BILL. Don't you mister me. You know my name, and I won't disgrace it when my time comes. Out with it.

FAGIN. Well then — Bill Skyes. You seem a little out of humor this mornin'.

BILL. Maybe I am.

FAGIN. Well, are you ready?

BILL. Ready for what?

FAGIN. No so loud. Somebody will hear us.

BILL. Let them then. *(But he lowers his voice a little anyhow.)* What do you want of me now?

FAGIN. Well, did you see the old Maylie place? What do you think now?

BILL. Oh, it's the job at Maylie's. Well, it can't be a put-up job, as we planned.

FAGIN. You don't tell me. Then you've bungled it somewhere.

BILL. Toby Crackit's been hanging about the place for a fortnight, and he can't get one of the servants into line.

FAGIN. You mean to tell me the women won't fall for a flash like Toby Crackit?

BILL. They simply won't have a thing to do with him.

FAGIN. He should have tried the mustachios and a canary waistcoat with military trousers.

BILL. He did, but they've been with the old lady these twenty years, and if you was to give 'em five hundred pounds, they wouldn't turn against her.

FAGIN. But it's got to be an inside job. You know that. The house is too well guarded to get in any other way. Someone has got to let us in.

BILL. Well — I tell you Mrs. Maylie's got 'em tied hand and foot, and they won't turn against her. Is — is it worth fifty shiners extra if I get in from the outside?

FAGIN. Now Bill, a bargain is a bargain.

BILL. Yes, but I promised to do it as an inside job, and it's worth fifty shiners extra if I get in from the outside. My job is housebreaking, and yours is picking pockets. Now you came to me and told me about the silver at the old Maylie place, and I agreed to get it for you. But I get it on my own terms, or not at all.

FAGIN. But you can't do it from the outside. I know that house. I've had my eye on that silver for months now.

BILL. Toby and me went over the garden wall last night. And we sounded all the doors and shutters. The place is shut up like a jail at night, but there is one place we can crack.

FAGIN. Where is it, Bill? Where is it?

BILL. If you knew that, you'd double-cross us and do it alone. It's best to be on the safe side when one deals with you.

FAGIN. Then why do you come here and say it can't be done?

BILL. I say it can't be done from the inside. And it's worth fifty shiners extra to take a chance from the outside. Then, too, we've got to have a boy.

FAGIN. Then it's a panel you're going to force. Or a window, maybe.

BILL. Never mind what it is, but I want a boy, and he mustn't be a big one, either. There ain't half a dozen boys left in the trade any more—thanks to the Juvenile Delinquent Society.

FAGIN. Nancy, my dear, will you just step in the next room and get my old pipe?

NANCY. Your old pipe is in your pocket where you always keep it. It ain't your pipe you want. I'm staying. Go on. Don't mind me.

BILL. Nancy ain't one to blab, Fagin. You know that.

NANCY. Go on, Fagin. Tell Bill about Oliver.

FAGIN. You're a clever one, Nancy. It was about Oliver I was going to speak. He's the boy for you. Bill. The others are too big.

NANCY. He's a new boy the Dodger brought in. A green one from the country.

FAGIN. He ain't so green. And once we let him feel he's one of us, he'll be one of us. Once we fill his mind with the idea that he's a thief, and he'll be a thief.

BILL. I must have a boy I can trust.

NANCY. He'll do what you tell him — if you scare him enough.

BILL. We won't need to scare him this time. It's a penny to a pound, Fagin, you'll never see that boy again. Think of that before you send him. If anything goes wrong, it will be the boy who gets it.

FAGIN. Well, well, it wouldn't be like losing one of the regular boys.

NANCY. When do you go, Bill?

BILL. Tonight. Where is this boy?

NANCY.   He's gone out with the Dodger. He'll be back any time now.

BILL.   *(Getting ready to leave. NANCY helps him with his scarf.)* You stay here, Nancy, and bring the boy home with you. If I'm not there, don't tell him what's up. And watch the dog. He don't like strangers.

(Bell rings.)

FAGIN.   That'll be the Dodger now. *(Goes to door.)* Who's there?

BILL.   All right. I'll wait and have a look at this Oliver myself.

DODGER.   *(Off.)* Plummy and slam.

FAGIN.   Come on up, Dodger. He's alone. They can't have got into trouble.

BILL.   Ah, the boy's behind him.

FAGIN.   I tell you he's alone. There wasn't but one step on the stairs. *(DODGER enters.)* Where's Oliver? *(Shaking him by the collar.)* Where's that boy? Speak, or I'll throttle you. Will you speak?

(He shakes him, but DODGER jerks away.)

DODGER.   The traps got him. Let me alone, I tell you.

FAGIN.   Where is that boy?

DODGER.   I told you. He's been arrested.

BILL.   What for?

DODGER.   There was an old cove at the book stall around the corner. and he looked like a prime plant if I ever saw one. So I just walked up close to him, and removed his handkerchief and turned to go, when there was Oliver, standing right close to me, all eyes. If I hadn't been in such a hurry, I'd 'a stopped to laugh right there. He's so jolly green, I never saw the like of it. And the old man turned around, and he must have suspected something, for he cried "Stop thief," and grabbed hold of Oliver. He got away, but they caught him again, and the last I seen, he was being carried away by the traps, and the old man was goin' with 'em, tryin' to explain how it happened.

FAGIN.   Oh, my poor boy. My poor little Oliver.

DODGER.   Ha! Your poor little boy! You poor little Oliver! My eye, what an old hypocrite you are.

BILL.   Someone must go to the jail and find out what's been done with him. We must get him back.

DODGER.   Why all the fuss? He'd never be of any use to us. I was a fool to bring him here in the first place.

FAGIN.   That boy is worth a hundred pounds to me. Bill's right. Someone must go to the jail. Nancy, my dear, what do you say?

NANCY.   It's no use tryin' that on me. I won't go.

FAGIN.   You're the very person. No one would suspect you.

NANCY.   And I don't want 'em to. Besides the boy's better off where he is.

BILL.   She'll go, Fagin.

NANCY.   No she won't, Fagin.

BILL.   Yes she will, Fagin.

NANCY.   *(Defies him for a moment, then gives in.)* All right. I'll go.

FAGIN.   Wait a minute, Nancy, *(Goes to pile of rags right and gets apron.)* Here, put this on. *(He gets a darker bonnet and shawl than her own.)* And these. They look more respectable than your own. *(She starts out.)* Stop a minute. Take this basket on your arm. And these keys. Now you look real and genuine. *(Stands off and rubs his hands.)* Very good, indeed. Not like our old Nancy at all, does she, Bill?

BILL.   She'll do. Now let's hear you try it. You go to the officers and ask for your little brother. Come on, let's have it.

NANCY.   Oh, my poor little brother. My poor, sweet, innocent little brother. What have you done with him? Where have you taken him? Oh, do have pity, gentlemen, and tell me what you have done with my poor, dear boy. Do, gentlemen, do — if you please.

(She breaks down and pretends to cry.)

FAGIN.   That's it. That's it. You are a clever girl, Nancy.

BILL.   Be off now. And mind you don't come back till you've found him.

(She starts for the door as the lights fade.)

End of Scene One

ACT ONE

Scene 2

The parlor of Mr. Brownlow's house. The room is well-furnished, and gives one the feeling that it belongs to people of refinement and culture. Above the fireplace hangs the painting of a beautiful girl. There is a marked resemblance between her and Oliver Twist.

OLIVER is discovered standing before the fire, looking at the picture. He is so interested in it, that he does not hear MRS. BEDWIN enters with a tea tray which she places on the table in front of the davenport. OLIVER is no longer the ragged Workhouse boy. He is well dressed, and has a bit of color in his face. MRS. BEDWIN adores OLIVER, and stands looking at him a moment before she speaks.

BEDWIN.   Well, well! You are fond of pictures, my dear.

OLIVER.   *(Starts and looks around.)* I — I don't know.

BEDWIN.   I didn't mean to scare you. Didn't you hear me come in?

OLIVER.   No ma'am, I didn't hear you.

BEDWIN.   What is it about that picture you like so much?

OLIVER.   The lady is so beautiful.

BEDWIN.   That's exactly what the artist wanted you to think. Painters always makes the ladies out prettier than they are. They are a deal more flattering than likenesses, I can tell you.

OLIVER.   Is that a — likeness, ma'am?

BEDWIN.   No, Oliver. That's a portrait.

OLIVER.   *(Not understanding.)* Oh. Who is the lady?

BEDWIN.   Bless me, I don't know. A friend of Mr. Brownlow's left it here a long time ago, and he never came back for it. It's hung upstairs for years, until you were sick, and you looked at it so much, the doctor thought it worried you. So Mr. Brownlow had it brought down here.

OLIVER.   *(Turns to face the picture.)* She's so lovely, it makes my heart beat — as if she were alive, and wanted to speak to me.

BEDWIN.   Lord save us! *(Feeling his forehead.)* Are you having fever again?

OLIVER.   No, I'm all right. But I'm glad I found her again.

BEDWIN. Like as not she's dead and gone to glory long ago. There are muffins for tea. Do you like them?

OLIVER. Muffins? I never had any.

BEDWIN. Never had muffins! Lord save us! Look here.

(She uncovers the plate.)

OLIVER. I like the smell, but we never had anything that smelled like that in the Workhouse.

BEDWIN. But you do like it here, don't you, Oliver?

OLIVER. It's like Heaven here. When I first woke up and saw you sitting by my bed, I thought I was dead and you were my mother— only she'd be younger than you are, I guess.

BEDWIN. It isn't polite to compare ladies' ages, Oliver.

OLIVER. I'm sorry, ma'am.

BEDWIN. Stuff and nonsense! I was only teasing you. *(She pats OLIVER'S shoulder. Picks up tea bell.)* Of course your mother would be much younger, and prettier, too. *(Going to the door, opens it, and rings the bell.)* Now when Mr. Brownlow comes down, we'll have tea. Tell him I'll be back directly. *(Exits.)*

OLIVER. All right, ma'am.

(He smells the muffins, ecstatically. Then he takes a book from the end of the davenport and sits on the fender, directly in front of the picture. MR. BROWNLOW now enters, and comes down to the fire. He is a dapper little man, who wears his clothes well; and looks every inch of a Dickens gentleman. OLIVER rises.)

BROWNLOW. So Bedwin got you downstairs at last, did she? Well, how do you feel today?

OLIVER. I've never felt so well, and I've never been so happy.

BROWNLOW. *(Looks from OLIVER to the picture.)* What's that! What's that!

OLIVER. What's what?

BROWNLOW. *(Pulls his spectacles down from his forehead and looks again.)* Well, well, well! I knew from the first there was something about you that— *(Lifts OLIVER'S face.)*

OLIVER. What is it, sir?

BROWNLOW. That's a remarkable likeness.

OLIVER. Mrs. Bedwin said it was a portrait, sir.

BROWNLOW. And so it is, but the likeness is between you, and the lady.

OLIVER. Do I look like her?

BROWNLOW. Haven't you ever seen yourself?

OLIVER. Once or twice, but I didn't look like that.

BROWNLOW. Well, you do now.

OLIVER. Maybe it's my new clothes.

BROWNLOW. Well, maybe. What are you reading?

OUVER. I wasn't reading. I — I just picked it up, sir.

BROWNLOW. That's all right. You may read anything in here you like. And across the hall is a room full of books.

OLIVER. There are a great many books, aren't there? I never knew there were so many. This one has a nice color.

BROWNLOW. I think you'll like reading them even better than looking at their outsides, though the covers are the best part of some books.

OLIVER. I suppose they are the heavy ones, sir.

BROWNLOW. Not always. How would you like to grow up and be a clever man, and write books, Oliver?

OUVER. Well, I think I'd rather read them, if you don't mind.

BROWNLOW. Well, we'll not make an author of you against your will. And now, Oliver, I think it's about time we had a talk. You're well enough now to hear what I have to say.

OLIVER. Oh, don't tell me that you are going to send me away from here. Don't send me out in the streets again. I'll be your servant. I'll do anything if you will only let me stay here. I can't go back to that wicked place where I came from, and I can't go back to the Workhouse, either.

BROWNLOW. I'll never send you back there, Oliver. You're all alone in the world, and so am I. And I like you. Now if you like me, I'll keep you here just as long as you want to stay, but first you must tell me more about yourself. Where did you come from?

OLIVIER. From the Workhouse, and then the undertaker's, and then walked to London.

BROWNLOW. I know all that, but after you came to London. Where were you before I brought you home from jail? Even in your fever, you wouldn't talk about that.

OLIVER. Oh sir, I can't tell you about that. They would kill me if I peached on them. The Dodger and Nancy said they would.

BROWNLOW. You needn't be afraid to tell me.

OLIVER. But I'm afraid. I wake up in the night, and I think I'm back there. Oh sir, if they ever get me again, they'll make a thief of —

BROWNLOW. So that's it.

OLIVER. What's it, sir?

BROWNLOW. So you were among thieves, and that boy who stole my handkerchief was one of your companions. *(The doorbell rings.)* Well, I won't press you any more today, Oliver, but think it over and make up your mind to tell me all about them.

(Offstage comes the booming voice of MR. GRIMWIG.)

GRIMWIG. *(Off.)* Good afternoon, Mrs. B. Good afternoon.

BEDWIN. *(Off.)* Good afternoon, Mr. Grimwig.

GRIMWIG. Are there muffins for tea?

BEDWIN. There are.

GRIMWIG. Then I'll stay. Help me off with my coat.

OLIVER. Shall I go upstairs again, sir?

BROWNLOW. No. Grimwig is an old friend, and I want him to know you.

GRIMWIG. Tell Mr. Brownlow that I am staying to tea.

BEDWIN. *(Appearing at door.)* If you haven't already heard, Mr. Grimwig is staying to tea.

GRIMWIG *(Entering.)* And muffins! I inquired first whether or not there would be muffins.

(He comes down center. His cane taps on the floor, and is often used to emphasize his none too gentle voice. He is large and red-faced, and as noisy as BROWNLOW is quiet. He too is well dressed, but his clothes are not so neat, nor so well worn. He dislikes BEDWIN, but this is mutual. And BROWNLOW is his one friend, although they argue constantly.)

BROWNLOW. You are always welcome, Mr.Grimwig.

GRIMWIG. And a fine welcome I had, too. *(Takes a piece of orange peel from his pocket.)* Look at this! A piece of orange peel on your step, sir. Isn't it a most wonderful and extraordinary thing that when I call at a man's house, I should find orange peel on the steps. I was made lame once by orange peel, and I know it will be my death. *(He notices OLIVER.)* Hallo, what boy is that?

BROWNLOW. This is Oliver Twist, whom we were speaking about. Oliver, this is Mr. Grimwig.

OLIVER. How do you do, sir?

GRIMWIG. You don't mean to say that's the boy who had the fever.

BROWNLOW. He's the very —

GRIMWIG. Stop! Don't speak! He's the very boy who had the orange peel, and left it on the steps for me to slip on. He's the very boy, or I'll eat his head. And mine, too.

BEDWIN. *(Indignantly.)* He hasn't had an orange, and he hasn't been out on the steps, either.

GRIMWIG. *(After glaring at her.)* So this is the boy you saved from jail, is it? Well, boy, how are you?

OLIVER. I'm a great deal better, sir.

BEDWIN. He has nice manners, hasn't he?

GRIMWIG. I don't know whether he has or not. I don't see much difference in boys. There are really only two kinds — mealy and beef-faced boys.

OLIVER. And which kind am I, sir?

GRIMWIG. Mealy. I knew a man once who had a beef-faced boy — a big, hulking creature, who was always bursting out at all seams. He was terrible.

BROWNLOW. Well, Oliver isn't like that.

GRIMWIG. He may be worse. He may be worse, I say. Who is he? Where does he come from? He hasn't been properly introduced, has he?

BROWNLOW. No, but —

GRIMWIG. No, but he's had a fever, and you and Mrs. B. are sorry for him. Well, that's no introduction. Fevers aren't particular. They attack bad boys as well as good ones.

BROWNLOW.   Come, come, Mr. Grimwig. Are we to suffer from your temper all afternoon? Just because you slipped on an orange peel that happened to be on my front steps —

GRIMWIG.   Happened to be on your front steps? Happened!

BROWNLOW.   Well, you don't think I put it there on purpose to trip you, do you?

GRIMWIG.   I haven't quite lost my good sense, sir. Put it there on purpose, indeed.

BROWNLOW.   Then let us say no more about it.

BEDWIN.   *(Taking up the muffins.)* Pass the muffins to Mr. Grimwig, Oliver.

OLIVER.   *(Crossing to him.)* Will you have some muffins, sir?

GRIMWIG.   Of course I'll have some muffins.

> *(He takes the plate which OLIVER holds, then takes one muffin, and then two, one at a time. OLIVER watches him, fearing he may take them all. He then goes to BROWNLOW.)*

BEDWLN.   *(To Brownlow.)* Tea for Mr. Grimwig.

OLIVER.   Will you have a muffin, sir?

BROWNLOW.   *(Taking one.)* Thank you.

BEDWIM.   I'll fix your palate, my dear. Now pass the preserves to Mr. Grimwig, Oliver.

> *(OLIVER takes the preserves to GRIMWIG.)*

GRIMWIG.   What flavor are they, ma'am?

BEDWIN.   Strawberry, sir.

GRIMWIG.   *(Again hesitating.)* Of your own preserving, ma'am?

BEDWIN.   I make all my own preserves. And my jellies, too.

GRIMWIG.   *(Takes generous helping.)* And very good they are, too — if I may say so, ma'am. *(Holding second spoonful.)* I'll bet you never had anything like that in the Workhouse, boy.

BROWNLOW.   Mr. Grimwig!

GRIMWIG.   Well, he came from the Workhouse, didn't he?

OLIVER.   Yes sir, I did, and we never had anything like this there, sir. Nor any muffins.

GRIMWIG.   What did you have?

OLIVER. Mostly gruel, sir. And twice a week we had onions. And a roll on Sunday.

GRIMWIG. No wonder you're so mealy.

BROWNLOW. Any then they starved you.

OLIVER. Well, I was hungry, but it wasn't so bad for me as it was for Dick.

BROWNLOW. Who was Dick?

OLIVER. Just a little boy in the Workhouse, but he's sick. I wanted him to run away too, but he wasn't strong enough to walk, and I couldn't carry him all the way to London. Some day I'm going back and get him.

BROWNLOW. We'll go the first warm day, Oliver.

GRIMWIG. *(Looks at picture over the fireplace.)* I never saw that before. Been wasting your money on pictures now, have you?

BROWNLOW. That belongs upstairs. I just brought it down here.

GRIMWIG. Who is she?

BROWNLOW. You remember Edwin Leeford?

GRIMWIG. Old Leeford's son? *(He nods.)* Made a bad marriage with some haughty, stuck-up thing. They had a son, and then separated. I remember.

BEDWIN. You always manage to remember the most unpleasant things about people.

GRIMWIG. They are always the most interesting, ma'am. *(To BROWNLOW.)* Did Leeford paint that?

BROWNLOW. Yes. He met that girl after he was separated from his wife, and fell in love with her. She was the daughter of an old naval officer, by the name of Fleming. When Leeford went to Rome on business, he left this picture with me. He died there, you remember, and it has been here ever since.

GRIMWIG. Did she get his money?

BROWNLOW. No, there was no will found, and the money went to your haughty-stuck-up thing, as you call her. She died too, but her son has probably made ducks and drakes of it by now.

BEDWLN. And that poor girl in the picture?

BROWNLOW. She disappeared after Leeford died, and they never found her. She had a sister, too — hardly more than a child at the time. I don't know what happened to her, either.

OLIVER. All the women at the Workhouse were so old and ugly. Nancy was pretty, but — well, not so clean.

BEDWIN. And who is Nancy?

OLIVER. Nancy is a girl I knew before I came here. I liked Nancy. She gave me sausages. But the Dodger and old Fagin… *(Stops suddenly.)*

GRIMWIG. The Dodger?

OLIVER. I didn't mean to say anything, sir.

GRIMWIG. Almost gave it away, didn't you? The Dodger! That sounds like thieves to me. Mr. Brownlow, you are a fool, and no mistake. The way this boy has taken you in.

BROWNLOW. Oliver will tell me all about it in his own good time. Mr. Grimwig, and I will not have him coerced.

GRIMWIG. Coerced the devil! Have you counted the spoons, Mrs. B?

BEDWIN. Mr. Grimwig needs another muffin, Oliver.

(The doorbell rings, and she goes to answer it. OLIVER passes the muffins again.)

GRIMWIG. I don't like that woman, Brownlow. Her tongue is sharp. But her muffins are tasty.

(He takes one, then replaces it and takes a larger one.)

BEDWIN. *(From the door.)* Your books have come, Mr. Brownlow.

BROWNLOW. Tell the boy to wait. There are some to go back.

BEDWIN. The boy has gone, sir.

BROWNLOW. Then call him back. Hurry. It's important. Don't let him get around the corner.

(He hurries out after her.)

OLIVER. *(After a silence, which he feels he must break.)* It's — it's very pleasant here, sir.

GRIMWIG. *(After a pause, and so loud he makes OLIVER jump.)* What's that?

OLIVER. *(Louder.)* I said it's very pleasant here.

GRIMWIG. I'm not deaf.

OLIVER. Mrs. Bedwin gives me cookies, and the doctor said I was to have all the milk I could drink.

GRIMWIG. And who pays for it, I'd like to know.

OLIVER. I never asked, sir.

GRIMWIG. No, no, of course not. I suppose you think Mr. Brownlow is made of money.

OLIVER. I never thought about it, but some day I'll pay him back for all the milk I drink.

GRIMWIG. And the clothes and the boots you wear. I warrant you didn't have those when you came here.

OLIVER. Oh no, you should have seen me then. Mr. Brownlow said I looked like a scarecrow, and Mrs. Bedwin fumigated me before she put me to bed. I was a sight. I didn't know it then, but I do now. Why, you get so used to dirt and rags in the poorhouse, that you don't know there is anything different until you come to a place like this. And then you wonder how you ever could have been so dirty. They used to wash us under the pump when the Board met, or Mr. Bumble was coming. Mr. Bumble was the Beadle, and he used to come to see us when we were bad. And one day he married Mrs. Corney. Mrs. Corney was a regular one—used to scold us all day, and beat us too. But the worst beating I ever got was when I bit Noah.

GRIMWIG. You bit Noah?

OLIVER. Yes, and I hit him too, because he called my mother names. And then I ran away and came to London.

GRIMWIG. And then?

OLIVER. And then Mr. Brownlow found me and brought me here.

GRIMWIG. So you don't mean to tell where you were before Mr. Brownlow found you.

OLIVER. No. Leastwise, I'll not tell you.

BROWNLOW. *(Entering.)* Dear, dear, that boy got away, and I wanted to return these books and pay for the ones I kept last time.

GRIMWIG. Why not send young Oliver with them. He will deliver them safely, you know.

OLIVER. Please let me take them, sir.

BROWNLOW. But you haven't been out of doors yet, and it's quite cold and almost dark.

OLIVER.   But I am well now, and I'd like to go, sir. I'd run all the way. Please let me go for you, sir.

BROWNLOW.   Are you sure you could go?

OLIVER.   Oh yes. I'd find the way.

GRIMWIG.   I haven't the slightest doubt of it.

BROWNLOW.   All right then, but you must be careful, and watch where you are going. Bedwin will tell you where to find the bookseller's. Tell her to wrap you up well, and here's a five-pound note to pay for the books he sent the other day. You are to pay four pounds ten, and bring me ten shillings change. You understand

OLIVER.   I give him four pounds ten, and bring you ten shillings change. Yes sir, I understand. Goodbye, Mr. Grimwig.

   (OLIVER exits.)

GRIMWIG.   And it is good bye, too.

BROWNLOW.   Don't worry. He'll be back in twenty minutes or so, and then we'll have dinner.

GRIMWIG.   I had every intention of staying to dinner, but you don't expect to see him again, do you?

BROWNLOW.   Don't you?

GRIMWIG.   I do not. He has new clothes on his back, a set of valuable books under his arm, and a five-pound note in his pocket. He'll go back to his old friends as fast as his legs can carry him, or I'll eat my head.

BROWNLOW.   I'll answer for his honesty with my life, sir.

GRIMWIG.   And I'd answer for his falsehood with my head. You saw him catch himself when he almost gave his precious friends away. He's deceiving you.

BROWNLOW.   *(Defiantly.)* We'll see.

GRIMWIG.   We will. We will.

BROWNLOW.   Did you notice the remarkable likeness between him and the girl in that picture?

GRIMWIG.   Now that you mention it, I do.

BROWNLOW.   I am convinced that she is the mother of that boy.

GRIMWIG.   Your imagination is running away with you.

BROWNLOW.   It is not impossible, sir. She disappeared, and her father died of a broken heart because he couldn't find her. I am determined to find out, for I believe Oliver is heir to half of Edwin Leeford's fortune.

GRIMWIG.   Mr. Brownlow, I say…that you are a sentimental old fool. How will you go about it?

BROWNLOW.   This first son of Leeford's was a bad lot, and when his mother — your haughty, stuck-up thing — died, he went to the West Indies. I'm going down there and find him and make him provide for the boy or know the reason why.

GRIMWTG.   Mr. Brownlow, I say again that you are a sentimental old fool, but if you are determined to make this journey, I will go with you.

BROWNLOW.   Mr. Grimwig! At your time of life?

GRIMWIG.   And what is the matter with my time of life? I can eat three meals a day, and digest them, too. And that's more than you can do. Say no more about it. I will go with you. And if you can prove that Oliver Twist is Edwin Leeford's son, and make that rascally brother give up half that money, I'll eat my head.

BROWNLOW.   That's a very handsome offer, Mr. Grimwig. And you may have to do it.

> *(The lights fade on them.)*

End of Scene Two

ACT ONE

Scene 3

Fagin's quarters.

The candles are lighted on the table, and the fire throws shadows. The DODGER sits on one side of the fire. He stirs something in a pot. FAGIN sits on the other side, crouching low over the fire. The DODGER tries to whistle, but it is a failure, he stops, sniffs, tastes the contents of the pan, then rises.

DODGER.   Fetch yourself a chair, Fagin. What's ailin' you, anyway? Mopin' around here like a sick cat.

FAGIN.   It's that boy, Dodger. I don't believe we'll ever get him back. It's weeks now, and we ain't heard a word from him.

DODGER. You'd better sent me to look for him. What does Nancy know about it?

FAGIN. Nancy's as smart as they make 'em, and a good actress too. If you found him, you'd let the cat out of the bag. I'd trust Nancy any day.

DODGER. Well, she ain't brought in the boy, has she? Just as you said, it's been weeks now.

FAGIN. And all that silver. And only two women in that old house. (*The bell rings.*) See who it is.

DODGER. (*At door.*) Who's there?

BILL. (*Off.*) Bill.

DODGER. What do you say?

BILL. Plummy and slam.

DODGER. Come up.

(*He does not close the door.*)

FAGIN. Who is it?

DODGER. It's Bill and Nancy.

BILL. Give us a light. We'll go breaking our legs.

DODGER. Stay where you are, and I'll get a light.

(*DODGE takes candle to the door and looks down.*)

BILL. Is the old 'un in there?

DODGER. Yes, and precious down in the mouth he is, too. Maybe you can cheer him up. Oh my wig! My wig! He's here! He's here! Fagin, look at him!

(*NANCY and BILL enter, with OLIVER between them.*)

FAGIN. Well, well, if it ain't Oliver come back again. We surely are glad to see you, my dear.

DODGER. (*Twirls OLIVER around.*) Oh Fagin, do look at him! Look at his togs! Oh my eye, what a game! And the books, Fagin! See the books. Nothing short of a gentleman, Fagin.

OLIVER. Let me alone.

FAGIN. We're delighted to see you looking so well, my dear. Why didn't you write and say you was comin' so we could have something hot for your supper?

OLIVER. You let me alone, I tell you.

DODGER. *(Pulls the five pound note from OLIVER'S pocket.)* My eye! Five pounds!

BILL. Hallo, what's that? *(He and FAGIN reach for it, but BILL gets it.)* It's mine, Fagin.

FAGIN. No, no, you can have the books.

OLIVER. Give me that money.

BILL. If this ain't mine, me and Nancy takes the boy back.

FAGIN. That's not fair, is it, Nancy?

BILL. Do you think Nancy has nothing else to do with her precious time but to follow every boy she's seen for weeks? Keep the books yourself if you're so fond of readin'. If not, you can sell 'em. You mouldy old miser.

OLIVER. Give me back the books, and give me back that money. It doesn't belong to me.

BILL. Who thought it did?

OLIVER. They belong to the gentleman who's been so kind to me. And he'll think I stole them. And the old lady will think so, too — and everybody. Give them back, I say!

BILL. Of course they'll think you stole them. And that's just what we want 'em to think.

FAGIN. It couldn't 'a happened better if we'd planned out a time to catch him.

BILL. I knowed that as soon as Nancy spotted him comin' along, with the books under his arm.

OLIVER. *(To BILL, his hand on BILL'S arm.)* Let me take them back. Please let me take them back. *(BILL throws his arm off.)* I'll do anything you say, if only you'll let me take them back.

FAGIN. Now then, Master Oliver, you might as well make up your mind to it. You're here, and you're here to stay.

OLIVER. Oh no, I'm not!

(He ducks into the DODGER, knocking him down, and makes for the open door, but BILL catches him and throws him back. He falls to the floor.)

BILL. No you don't. Not with Bill Sykes watchin' you, you don't. Dodger, shut that door and lock it. You was a fool to leave it open. Fagin, bring your whip. I'll teach him to try to run away.

> *(FAGIN goes to the fireplace and takes down a heavy whip. NANCY springs between SYKES and OLIVER.)*

NANCY. You shan't strike him, Bill.

BILL. *(Pushing her away.)* Keep out of this, Nancy, or I'll show you who's master here.

NANCY. I don't care. I don't care what you do to me, but you shan't strike Oliver.

FAGIN. What's the matter with you, Nancy?

> *(He extends the whip to BILL, but NANCY bars the way.)*

BILL. *(Throws NANCY out of the way.)* Get out of my way! *(OLIVER starts toward NANCY. BILL addresses him directly.)* So you wanted to get away, did you? Wanted to call the police, did you? Well I'll cure you of that notion.

NANCY. *(Grasping BILL'S arm.)* I won't stand by and see it done, Bill. I got the boy back for you. Now let him be. Let him be, I tell you.

FAGIN. Why Nancy, you're cleverer than ever tonight. You're acting better than ever.

NANCY. Take care I don't overdo it. You'll be the worse for it if I do. *(She snatches the whip as FAGIN tries to pass it to BILL.)* No you don't Bill.

> *(NANCY throws the whip into the fire, and stands defiantly before it.)*

BILL. *(Advancing on her.)* Do you know what you're about?

NANCY. Yes I do, and I won't stand by and see that child mistreated.

BILL. You're a nice one to turn humane and genteel. You're a nice friend for that child, as you call him.

NANCY. Yes, God help me, I am. I wish I'd been struck dead in the street before I lent a hand to bringing him back here.

BILL. *(Snatching her by the arm.)* I've had enough of this.

NANCY. *(Wincing but standing her ground.)* I mean what I say, Bill. Don't you strike Oliver.

FAGIN. *(Sees how desperate she is.)* Come, come. Bill, let her off this time, and we'll let the boy off, too, if he does what we tell him. Let's have civil words now, Nancy, and no more quarrelin'.

NANCY. Civil words! Civil words, you old villain. You deserve them from me, don't you? Haven't I thieved for you since I was a child not half as old as he? Haven't I been in the same trade and in the same service for twelve years? Don't you know it? Speak! Don't you know it?

FAGIN. Well, well, and what if you have? Isn't it your living?

NANCY. Yes, it's my living. And the wet dirty streets are my home, and you're the one who put me there. And you'll keep me there, day and night, till the day I die.

FAGIN. There, there, Nancy, you're all unstrung. And like as not, the whole place is aroused by now. Go outside and watch the stairs, Dodger. If you hear anyone down below, give us the word.

(DODGER goes out, and BILL locks the door.)

BILL. I'll let you off this time, but if you try any more tricks with me, you'll get all that's comin' to you, and more. You understand? *(OLIVER nods. BILL turns to FAGIN.)* Come on in here, Fagin. I want to talk to you.

FAGIN. I know, I know. I got 'em all ready for you.

(They go out left. OLIVER kneels beside NANCY.)

OLIVER. Nancy, Nancy dear, please don't cry so. I'll never forget the way you stood up for me, Nancy. Never! It was like being at Mr. Brownlow's again, and knowing that somebody cared what happened to you. Oh, Nancy, they were so good to me there. For the first time in all my life, someone wanted me, and tried to make me happy.

NANCY. And I brought you back here. But I never thought it would be like this. And I had to do it.

OLIVER. I'm not blaming you, Nancy. I know you had to do it. You have to do everything they tell you. That's why it was so splendid, the way you stood up for me. *(She shivers and draws away.)* What's the matter, Nancy? Are you cold?

NANCY. No, it's the shivers. They come over me sometimes.

OLIVER. Why did you bring me back, Nancy?

NANCY. You'll have to go with Bill tonight, Oliver.

OLIVER. What for?

NANCY. No harm, I hope.

OLIVER. I don't believe that, Nancy.

NANCY. Well, for no good, then. But you'll have to go. I can't help you any more, and you can't help yourself either. They're too strong for us. We're hedged around on all sides.

OLIVER. I will get away, Nancy, you must come too.

NANCY. You heard what Bill said, and the Dodger is on guard out there. If you ever get away from them, this is not the time, Oliver.

OLIVER. *(Rising to look at the skylight.)* The skylight, Nancy. We could get over the roofs, maybe. We could put a chair on the table, and —

NANCY. Ssshhh! They'll hear, Oliver. And every word they hear means a blow for both of us now. They'd never believe I didn't try to help you.

OLIVER. But Nancy, I can't stay here and do nothing. I can't let them force me out to steal for them. If I hadn't been with Mr. Brownlow, it might have been different, but I won't be a thief now. I won't!

NANCY. *(Putting her hand over his mouth.)* They mustn't ever hear you say that, Oliver. I saved you once tonight, but I can't do it again.

OLIVER. But I will get away, and the next time. I'll peach on them too.

NANCY. Do you want them to beat me too, Oliver?

OLIVER. No, no, I'll stay, Nancy. I'll do anything you say. Tell me what they want me to do tonight.

NANCY. Bill will tell you fast enough.

OLIVER. Just a word, Nancy. Just a hint.

NANCY. *(Draws him closer and speaks lower.)* Well, there's an old house to be robbed. It was planned for the night you disappeared, but they needed a boy. That's the reason they wanted you back. They'll force a window. You are to crawl in and unlock the door for them. There's only an old lady and her niece, and some old servants. You go with 'em, Oliver, and when you're once in the house, you find some way to turn on them and save yourself. That's the only way you'll ever escape now.

OLIVER. I will, Nancy, and some day I'll come back and take you away too.

NANCY. It's too late for me now, Oliver.

OLIVER. No, I'd go back to Mr. Brownlow and tell him about you. He'd believe you, and he'd help you too.

NANCY. No, Oliver, don't peach on them, whatever you do. They'd never let you alone after that. They'd hunt you down to the last day you lived. Get away if you can, but don't try to help me. I've been here too long. Shh! They're coming back now.

(She pushes OLIVER away, and turns her back on him. BILL enters, followed by FAGIN. He goes to the table, and lays down a large pistol.)

BILL. *(To OLIVER.)* Come here. *(OLIVER goes slowly to him.)* Do you know what this is?

OLIVER. I do.

BILL. Well then, look here. This is powder…and that's a bullet …and this little piece of old hat is for waddin'. *(Puts it in gun.)* Now it's loaded, see?

OLIVER. Yes, I see it.

BILL. Well, you speak a word tonight, except when I speak to you. And that load will be in your head. Without notice. So if you do make up your mind to speak without leave, you'd better say your prayers; first. Understand?

NANCY. He means if you try to double-cross him. he'll shoot you, and take his chances of swingin' for it afterwards.

BILL. That's it. Now you understand?

OLIVER. Yes, I understand.

BILL. Come along then. Let's get going.

FAGIN. Don't you be afraid, my dear. We ain't sendin' you into no danger. Do just what Bill tells you, and whatever falls out. Mind you don't say a word.

BILL. Hold your din. Come along now.

(OLIVER turns to NANCY, but she will not look at him. He goes to her.)

OLIVER. Nancy.

NANCY. *(Coldly.)* Go along with Bill now, and do what he tells you, like Fagin says.

OLIVER. Good bye, Nancy.

(She looks at him for a moment, then turns away to the fire. He goes to the door and joins BILL. Once he turns back and looks at her, but BILL gives him a push out of the door, then follows him. FAGIN locks the door after them.)

FAGIN. Well, Nancy.

(Then he goes to the table, tastes the rabbit pie, licks his lips, draws up a chair, and starts to eat in earnest as the lights fade.)

End of Act One

ACT TWO

Scene 1

Fagin's quarters, the next morning.

A violent storm is raging outside. NANCY sits at the table with some mending, but she works by fits and starts. FAGIN crouches by the fire, as before.

FAGIN.   The Dodger will be wet through. I don't see what's keeping him. *(The bell rings.)* There, that'll be him now. Open the door, Nancy.

NANCY.   *(At the door.)* Who's there?

DODGER.   *(Off.)* It's me, the Dodger.

NANCY.   Come up, then. And be quick about it, for that wind blows out all the candles. *(She holds the door against the wind.)* It's him, the Dodger.

(DODGER enters, and he is plainly uneasy. She closes the door. FAGIN looks up.)

FAGIN.   Well — well?

DODGER.   *(Hanging up his hat.)* Hallo.

FAGIN.   What is it? Tell me.

DODGER.   Well, first and foremost —

FAGIN.   It's bad news. I know it when you use that tone. Well, out with it.

DODGER.   I just seen Toby Crackit.

NANCY.   Alone? Where's Bill?

DODGER.   I — I don't know.

FAGIN.   Don't keep anything back now. Tell us what Toby said.

DODGER.   There's nothing to keep back. Toby doesn't know anything. He asked me about Bill.

FAGIN. Do you mean to say — Where is Bill and that boy? They're hiding somewhere.

DODGER. Well, Toby Crackit don't know any more than we do. The robbery was a failure, though.

FAGIN. I thought so. What else?

DODGER. They got into the house, all right, but the servants fired and hit him.

NANCY. Not Bill! They didn't hit Bill!

DODGER. No, the boy — Oliver. Toby and Bill got out all right, and cut across the fields back of the house, with the boy between 'em. But the whole countryside was aroused, and they had the dogs on 'em too. It was each man for himself, so they left the boy in a ditch and ran for it. They lost sight of each other, and Toby made his way back to London. He's been layin' low ever since.

FAGIN. And Oliver? What became of him?

DODGER. I told you they left him in a ditch — dead or alive, I don't know.

FAGIN. Poor little chil— left in a ditch. Only think of it, Nancy.

NANCY. It's Bill I'm thinkin' of. The boy is better off if he died in the ditch.

FAGIN. You don't mean that, Nancy.

NANCY. Yes I do. I'd be glad to know that the worst is over for him. The sight of him turned me against myself, and against all of you, too.

DODGER. Pooh! You're on edge tonight. It's the storm.

FAGIN. If Bill comes back without that boy, I'll make him pay for it.

NANCY. Bill warned you. He said if anything happened, it would be the boy who got it.

FAGIN. He's left him in the ditch. And that boy is worth a hundred pounds to me. Now what will I say to Monks tonight?

NANCY. Is Monks coming here tonight?

FAGIN. He's due now. Oh, it's bad enough for Bill to lose me all that old silver. But the boy too —

NANCY. If Bill's failed this time, he's done many a good job for you, and he'll do many another. As for the boy, he had to take his chance with the rest, and I say again that I hope he's dead and out of harm's way, and yours too.

(NANCY starts to exit.)

FAGIN. Where are you goin', Nancy?

NANCY. I'm goin' home. Bill might be there.

DODGER. He wasn't there this afternoon.

NANCY. But he might be there now. If Toby Crackit got back to London, why so could Bill. He's worth two of Toby, any day.

DODGER. You'll be wet to the skin.

NANCY. It wouldn't be the first time.

FAGIN. You go with her, Dodger. It's late for Nancy to be out alone.

NANCY. He can stay here. I don't want him.

DODGER. That's all right with me. I'm not keen to go out again tonight.

FAGIN. If Nancy won't have you, you'd better stop by the Three Cripples. Bill might have turned up there.

DODGER. I stopped there this morning.

FAGIN. Well, well, it's been a long time since morning. Get along now. *(Pulls him from the table, pushes him toward door.)* And mind what you. say, too. We mustn't seem too anxious about Bill.

DODGER. Why don't you go yourself, if you're so anxious to know?

FAGIN. I can't go out on a night like this. And besides, I'm expecting Monks.

DODGER. And you want us out of the way before he comes.

FAGIN. Well, Monks ain't too sociable. Get along now.

DODGER. Come along, Nancy.

FAGIN. Better leave the door open, so you can see your way down. I'll close it after you in a minute.

(He goes into the other room.)

NANCY. You go on Dodger. I want to get something first.

DODGER. *(As he exits.)* Dirty old hound! Sending me out again on a night like this.

(He is gone. NANCY looks about uncertainly, runs to the table and blows out the candle. Then she hides under the rags. The room is in darkness. FAGIN enters. Lightning.)

FAGIN.   Drat that wind. I might have known it would blow out the candles. *(He stumbles about in the dark.)* I'll break my old shins before I find another one. Next time, I'll let them break their necks on the stairs. *(He lights another candle from the fire, and places it in a bottle on the table, then goes to the door and closes it, and returns to his place by the fire. The bell rings.)* That'll be Monks now. Got 'em out just in time. *(He listens.)* No, there's three of 'em. Couldn't be Bill and the boy. *(Goes toward door.)* Must't bumped into Nancy and the Dodger down there. *(Opens the door.)* Who's there? I can't hear for the wind. That you, Monks…Who's with you? Don't like strangers — not on a night like this. Or any other time, for that matter. *(Knock on the door.)* Come in, Monks.

(He opens the door, and MONKS enters, followed by MR. and MRS. BUMBLE. MR. BUMBLE is heavy, past middle-age, with small, watery eyes and a red face. MRS. BUMBLE is tall and spare, with a hard, efficient look. They are both dressed for the weather.)

MONKS. Mr. and Mrs. Bumble. I have a little business to discuss with them. Do you mind?

FAGIN.   They're welcome, I'm sure. Bumble, did you say?

BUMBLE.   Good old family name. Bumble. I didn't catch your name.

MONKS.   Names aren't important here. *(The BUMBLES exchange glances.)* We're wet as rats. Can't you give us something hot?

FAGIN.   Just a minute, Monks. Sit down, ma'am. Over there, by the table. Sit down, Mr. Bumble. Some hot ale would warm you up, I reckon. Have some right here. Always keep it on a night like this. Bring the mugs from the cupboard, Monks.

MRS. BUMBLE.   *(In a low tone, to her husband.)* Mind what I tell you. Let me do the talkin' here. I don't like the looks of this place, or the men either.

MONKS.   *(To FAGIN.)* Any of the others in there?

FAGIN.   No. Whatever do you mean, bringin' 'em up here. You know I don't like strangers.

MONKS.   I hadn't any place else to take them, and if you ever say a word about what goes on here tonight —

FAGIN.   You can trust me, Monks. You know that.

MONKS. All right — all right. Now warm them up. I want them to talk.

FAGIN. *(Giving them ale.)* Here you are, ma'am. Here sir. That'll stop your teeth chatterin'.

MRS. BUMBLE. Now sir, perhaps you'll tell us why you brought us here on a night like this.

MONKS. I want to take your minds back twelve years ago — on a night like this. You were matron of the Workhouse then, I think?

BUMBLE. Aye, but she was Mrs. Corney then.

MONKS. That's nothing to do with it. A boy was born that night.

MRS. BUMBLE. I don't know what you mean. There's been a lot of boys born in the Workhouse in my time.

BUMBLE. Yes, little dears.

(MRS. BUMBLE nudges him to be still.)

MONKS. I mean the one you apprenticed to a coffin-maker, and who afterwards ran away.

BUMBLE. Ah, he means Oliver — little Oliver Twist. Now there was a rascal for you. I had my hands full with him, I can tell you.

MONKS. I am trying to discuss this matter with your wife. What became of the old hag who nursed his mother?

MRS. BUMBLE. Old Mrs. Thingummy died last winter.

MONKS. So much the better. She's out of the way.

(BUMBLE begins to speak, but is checked by his wife.)

MRS. BUMBLE. You didn't get us up here on a night like this to ask about old Mrs. Thingummy.

MONKS. No. Blast that lightning! How I hate the sight of it

BUMBLE. Now I had a cow once who couldn't stand lightning either. Used to —

MRS. BUMBLE. Hold your tongue, Bumble. Well sir, let's get clown to business.

MONKS. Yes, the sooner we get down to business, the better.

MRS. BUMBLE. Before we go on, how much is this information worth to you?

MONKS. How can I tell until I know what it is?

MRS. BUMBLE.   You think a woman can't keep a secret. Well, I know when to talk and when to keep still.

MONKS.   Come, come, Mrs. Bumble. We'll not fall out over a little money. I'll pay for the information.

MRS. BUMBLE.   Well, what is it worth to you?

MONKS.   It may be worth nothing. It may be worth twenty pounds.

FAGIN.   Twenty pounds! Now Monks, that's too much.

MRS. BUMBLE.   Give me five and twenty, and I'll tell you.

FAGIN.   *(Almost crying.)* Five and twenty? Monks!

MRS. BUMBLE.   I spoke as plain as I could, and it's not a large sum, either. *(BUMBLE is about to speak.)* Now keep still, Bumble, and let me handle this. *(To MONKS.)* Well, do I get it?

MONKS.   Five and twenty! H'mm.

MRS. BUMBLE.   *(Stands, draws her shawl up, as if to go.)* Well, I always say old secrets are like old wine. They improve with age.

MONKS.   And I may be paying for nothing.

MRS. BUMBLE.   Well, you could always take it back. I'm only a woman, and unprotected here.

BUMBLE.   You forget that I am here, my dear. I'm not so young as I was, and a little gone to seed, maybe, but I've been an officer of the law in my day. And I was a determined officer of the law, with very uncommon strength when I was aroused. I only want a little arousing, that's all.

(MRS. BUMBLE sits.)

MONKS.   I'll give you the money, but mind you make it worth my while. Old Mrs. Thingummy had something that belonged to Oliver's mother, and she gave it to you when she died.

MRS. BUMBLE.   How did you know that?

MONKS.   Some of the old women at the Workhouse knew about it.

MRS. BUMBLE.   I was alone with old Thingummy when she died. They couldn't know.

MONKS.   No, they couldn't. But they did. Now — what did she do with it?

MRS. BUMBLE.   She sold it.

MONKS.   Where? When? To whom? No, no, she gave you something that night.

MRS. BUMBLE.   She gave me a pawnbroker's ticket. I redeemed it.

MONKS.   Where is it?

MRS. BUMBLE.   Put your money on the table first. I'll not sell until I see your money.

MONKS.   *(Counting out the money.)* You drive a hard bargain, Mrs. Bumble. There you are.

MRS. BUMBLE.   *(Takes out a small bag and places it on the table.)* And there you are.

MONKS.   *(Taking out contents.)* A locket and wedding ring.

MRS. BUMBLE.   With Agnes on the inside of it.

MONKS.   Is that all?

MRS. BUMBLE.   Yes, that's all. Can they be used against me in any way — keeping them, I mean?

MONKS.   No, and they'll be at the bottom of the river tonight, when I leave here. Now we may as well break up this little party. *(To BUMBLE.)* I can trust your wife. She knows when to talk. But how about you?

BUMBLE.   You can count on me, sir. Why, in all the years I was an officer of the law, I —

MONKS.   All right, all right. Now get away from here as quick as you can, and forget it.

(FAGIN goes to open the door for them.)

BUMBLE.   *(Offering his arm to MRS. BUMBLE, and leading her toward the door.)* Come, my love. Our room is worth more than our company. *(Turns to FAGIN.)* Good night to you, Mr. — er—

FAGIN.   *(Showing them out.)* Good night, ma'am. Watch your steps. They're a little worn. *(Closing the door after them.)* Well, well, you have done it now. Twenty-life pounds for an old locket. *(Examines the locket.)* It ain't worth it, Monks. You've been cheated.

MONKS.   *(Putting ring and locket together away.)* It's worth it to me. Now where's that boy?

FAGIN.   I — I don't just know.

MONKS.   What do you mean, you don't know. Has he got away again?

FAGIN. Well, in a manner of speakin' — yes.

MONKS. I might have known you'd bungle things. How did it happen this time?

FAGIN. He went on a job with Bill and Toby, and they ain't got back yet.

MONKS. That won't do. I saw Toby today.

FAGIN. But Bill and the boy ain't come yet.

MONKS. Where did they go?

FAGIN. To the country. To that old Maylic house in Chertsey.

MONKS. What!

FAGIN. Ah, you know the place? Well, the robbery failed, and the boy was — hit.

MONKS. Killed?

FAGIN. I don't think so, but they left him in a ditch near the house.

MONKS. And the old lady and Rose took him in and cared for him.

FAGIN. I tell you I don't know what happened to him.

MONKS. That's what happened, all right. You can depend on it. Mrs. Maylie and Rose are that kind. It's the devil's own luck to have him fall into their hands.

FAGIN. Friends of yours, maybe?

MONKS. I've had my eye on that girl Rose for years. Why didn't you keep him here and make a pickpocket out of him, like the others? In a year at least, he would have been convicted and sent out of the country.

FAGIN. And whose turn would that have served?

MONKS. Mine.

FAGIN. And what about mine? It takes two to make a bargain.

MONKS. I told you I'd pay you.

FAGIN. You said you wanted him to be a thief, and out of the way too. Well, if he's alive, I'll make a thief out of him. And if he's dead, why he's out of the way, ain't he?

MONKS. We must make sure of that. If old Maylie knew who he is, she'd give a thousand pounds. But the only proof of his identity will lie at the bottom of the river tonight, and the old hag who nursed his mother is in her coffin. I've got his money sewed up all right now, and if he is still living, I'll make a criminal out of him, and complete the terms of that will. Thief as you are, Fagin, you've never set such snares as I will contrive for my brother Oliver.

FAGIN. Little Oliver your brother! Now I see —

MONKS. I was a fool to tell you that.

FAGIN. You can trust me, Monks.

MONKS. And pay you double, now that you know my secret. You crafty old weasel! It's a wonder some of your boys haven't done for you long ago.

FAGIN. Why, they love me. Old Fagin's boys, they calls themselves.

MONKS. Well, they're welcome. Let me out of here. It's stifling. Bring a light. *(Opens door and starts out.)* You'll have to come down part way. I don't intend to break my neck.

(FAGIN follows him out. NANCY rises from the pile of rags, and looks wildly about the room. She goes to the door and listens, then she closes and leans again it. FAGIN is heard outside grumbling. She runs to the door left, drops her shawl without noticing it, and closes the door after her.)

FAGIN. Might have known that wind would close the door. *(He locks the door again.)* Such a night. *(He steps on Nancy's shawl, and stoops to pick it up.)* Hallo, what's this? Nancy's been hidin' here again. Nancy! Nancy! *(NANCY opens the door. She yawns and seems half asleep.)* What are you doin' in there?

NANCY. *(Yawning.)* I — I went to sleep, I guess.

FAGIN. You didn't pass me on the stairs, and your shawl ain't even been damp. You couldn't 'a been in there all this time. You ain't been out of this room. *(He looks about the room, working toward the rag pile.)* You was hidin' here — in his room. So! You was under the rags, was you?

NANCY. *(Taking her shawl.)* Ah, let me alone.

FAGIN. Where are you goin' now?

NANCY. I've got to get out of here.

FAGIN. Where are you goin'?

NANCY. Not far.

FAGIN. That's no answer. Where are you goin', I say?

NANCY. And I say not far.

FAGIN. And I say where. Do you hear me?

NANCY.   I don't know where.

FAGIN.   *(Pushes her toward chair.)* That you don't. Sit down. You ain't goin' nowhere tonight.

NANCY.   I want some air.

FAGIN.   Stick your head out of the window then.

NANCY.   Let me go. I'll be back in an hour. I promise.

FAGIN.   Sit down, Nancy. *(She does.)* Now you heard every word in this room tonight. Once before, you listened to what Monks had to tell me about Oliver. You're sorry for that boy, and you want to help him. But you know what happens to the one who peaches. You know the law of our trade.

NANCY.   You'd do for me. I know that. Don't think I don't. I ain't been around here for twelve years without seein' it happen.

FAGIN.   Well, don't say I didn't warn you.

NANCY.   I know what I'm doing. I'll think a long time before I peach on you. Between you and Bill, I wouldn't stand a chance, I guess.

FAGIN.   All right, Nancy. You can go now. *(She goes out, and he locks the door and goes toward the table. Suddenly he thinks of the watches, and runs to the rags to hunt for them. He emerges with the red leather box, brings it to the table, opens it, and. sits.)* No, no, they're all here. She didn't take nothing. Fine fellows, every one of 'em…and they didn't peach on old Fagin.

   (The lights fade.)

ACT TWO

Scene 2

Brownlow's house, several months later.

BROWNLOW and GRIMWIG are discovered, BROWNLOW sitting next to the fire on the end of the davenport, GRIMWIG on the other end.

BROWNLOW.   *(Rising and going toward the table with a book.)* Well, well, we'll say no more about it.

GRIMWIG.   *(Moving into the place next the fire.)* There's nothing like an English fireside at my time of life. You couldn't induce me to take another ocean voyage.

BROWNLOW. And I couldn't induce you to remain in England when I went to the Indies.

GRIMWIG. I could hardly see you go on that fool's errand alone.

BROWNLOW. I don't know what help you were. And the fool's errand has resulted in one thing at least. I've traced that rascal Leeford back to London.

GRIMWIG. And lost him again like a needle in a haystack.

BROWNLOW. And found him again. Two days ago, I spoke to him on the street. He turned and ran, but I have men looking for him who will bring him here the moment he is found.

GRIMWIG. What good will it do you, now that you've lost Oliver?

BROWNLOW. I'll find Oliver too, and that's not all. I've located the matron of that Workhouse. She's coming to see me, too.

GRIMWIG. How much further has this obsession led you?

BROWNLOW. To South Wales, where that Captain Fleming and his daughters lived. But all I learned there was that the younger one was adopted by a rich old lady.

(*Bell rings.*)

GRIMWIG. And now I suppose you'll be chasing after the rich old lady.

BROWNLOW. If I knew her name, I would.

GRIMWIG. (*Rising.*) I hesitate to say it, Mr. Brownlow, but I am beginning to think you are of unsound mind.

BROWNLOW. Mr. Grimwig!

(*BEDWIN enters.*)

BEDWIN. (*Giving BROWNLOW a card.*) A young gentleman and a lady to see you, sir.

BROWNLOW. (*Reading the card.*) Harry Maylie. I don't know any Maylie. (*To BEDWIN.*) Well, well, don't stand there. Show them in. (*She goes out. He gives the card to GRIMWIG.*) Maylie? What do you make of it?

GRIMWIG. There's a family by that name in Chertsey—an old lady and her son, I think. Maybe there is a daughter too. I don't just remember. But there was a robbery down there about the time we went to the Indies.

BROWNLOW. Dear, dear! A robbery! What can they want of me?

(BEDWIN enters with HARRY MAYLIE and ROSE. He is young, good looking, and well-dressed in the fashion of the period. She is a beautiful girl, of seventeen, and very slight for her age. She too is well-dressed, and her eyes shine with excitement.)

BEDWIN. Mr. Brownlow will see you.

HARRY. Thank you. Mr. Brownlow?

BROWNLOW. I am at your service, Mr. Maylie.

HARRY. *(Introducing ROSE.)* My sister, Miss Rose.

BROWNLOW. And my friend, Mr. Grimwig. Miss Rose. Mr. Maylie.

HARRY. *(Bowing.)* How do you do, sir?

GRIMWIG. *(Making a most elaborate bow.)* Your most obedient…If I am in the way, Mr. Brownlow, I will retire.

ROSE. *(Sitting in armchair, which Mr. BROWNLOW holds for her.)*. Please don't go, Mr. Grimwig. I think you too will be interested in what we have come to tell you.

> *(BROWNLOW places chair near her for HARRY, and goes back to the davenport himself.)*

GRIMWIG. *(Rising and bowing again to ROSE.)* Your most obedient, ma'am.

ROSE. Mr. Brownlow, we have come to see you about Oliver Twist.

BROWNLOW. Oliver Twist! God bless my soul!

GRIMWIG. So he's turned up again. There's a bad one, or I'll eat my head.

ROSE. He's a dear, sweet child, and would do honor to men six times his age.

GRIMWIG. I'm sixty-one, and if that remark was intended to be personal, I fail to see the application, young lady.

> *(ROSE gasps.)*

BROWNLOW. Don't pay any attention to him. He doesn't mean a thing he says.

GRIMWIG. Yes he does.

BROWNLOW. No he doesn't.

GRIMWIG. He'll eat his head if he doesn't.

BROWNLOW. He deserves to have it knocked off if he does.

GRIMWIG. *(Rises.)* And he would uncommonly well like to see the man who offers to do it.

BROWNLOW. *(Rising also.)* Mr. Grimwig. *(They shake hands, and sit again. ROSE and HARRY are convulsed.)* Now Miss Maylie, what have you to tell me?

ROSE. You remember Oliver?

BROWNLOW. Remember him? I'll never forget him. *(GRIMWIG is about to speak, but BROWNLOW silences him.)* Mr. Grimwig.

  (GRIMWIG subsides with a grunt.)

ROSE. He's never forgotten you, either. Mr. Brownlow.

GRIMWIG. He wouldn't.

HARRY. He came to us by way of an accident. My mother's house in Chertsey was broken into last winter.

GRIMWIG. Didn't I tell you he would go back to those —

  (BROWNLOW glares at him.)

HARRY. One of our servants shot in the dark, and hit Oliver.

BROWNLOW. He—he isn't dead?

ROSE. No, it was only a flesh wound in the arm.

GRIMWIG. I always said that boy was a thief.

ROSE. But Oliver isn't a thief. The real thieves made him crawl in to open the door for them. They escaped, but we found him next morning in a ditch. He was ill for weeks.

GRIMWIG. It's a most wonderful and extraordinary thing how some boys can always manage to have an attack of fever.

HARRY. *(To BROWNLOW.)* He was out of his head for several weeks, but as soon as he regained consciousness he insisted that you must be found. He wanted you to know that the thieves caught him on the way to the bookseller's, took your books and money, and that night they brought him down to Chertsey for the robbery.

ROSE. We tried to find you then, but you had gone to the West Indies.

BROWNLOW. And so I had. You've brought me great happiness, young lady, but you haven't yet told me where to find Oliver.

HARRY. Why Oliver and my mother are waiting in the coach at the door.

BROWNLOW. *(Rises.)* At this very door? At my door, sir?

HARRY. Yes, we thought we'd better—

(But he talks to the air. BROWNLOW has rushed out and HARRY follows him.)

GRIMWIG. *(Goes to ROSE.)* You're a nice girl, and I like you.

(Unexpectedly, he kisses her. She gasps.)

ROSE. Well, of all—

GRIMWIG. Tush! Tush! I'm old enough to be your grandfather.

(He goes out. She gets up and looks at the portrait.)

ROSE. Why, where have I—

(GRIMWIG re-enters with MRS. MAYLIE, a frail, aristocratic old lady who is so startled that she hardly knows where she is.)

GRIMWIG. Come right over here to the fire, ma'am.

MRS. MAYLIE. Well, of all the unceremonious—

(HARRY comes in after them, laughing.)

GRIMWIG. You must be half-frozen, sitting out there in the coach all this time. There now. Sit down. *(He puts her down on the davenport.)* And put your feet on the fender. *(He places her feet on the fender, and she arranges her dress.)* Now, I'll fetch you a nip of something hot.

(He hurries off.)

MRS. MAYLIE. *(Indignantly.)* Harry! Rose! I'm all flustered. I don't understand.

(HARRY laughs.)

ROSE. *(Sits beside her.)* What's happened?

MRS. MAYLIE. Oliver and I were sitting quietly in the coach outside, when the door to this house flew open, and a little man rushed down the steps like a whirlwind. And then came that great hulking fellow. He's a tornado. He bundled me into the house like a bag of salt.

HARRY. Oh, it's all right, Mother. They're just excited about finding Oliver.

OLIVER. *(As he and BROWNLOW enter.)* I couldn't have waited much longer, sir. If you hadn't come when you did—*(Stops as he meets GRIMWIG, entering with a small glass of whiskey.)* How do you do, Mr. Grimwig.

GRIMWIG. *(Shakes OLIVER'S hand and lets it drop quickly.)* Well, boy, you're not so mealy as you were the last time I saw you.

OLIVER. Oh no, sir. I've had a summer in the country.

GRIMWIG. And more new clothes, I see. It's a marvelous and extra ordinary thing how the Lord looks after some boys.

MRS. MAYLIE. The Lord didn't do it all, Mr. Grimwig.

GRIMWIG. *(Goes to her and presents whiskey.)* Hot toddy, ma'am? Hot toddy?

MRS. MAYLTE. Thank you, but I don't need your hot toddy.

GRIMWIG. Take it, ma'am. It will settle your stomach.

(ROSE takes it and holds it for MRS. MAYLIE. BEDWIN enters.)

BEDWIN. Did you call me, sir?

BROWNLOW. I did.

BEDWIN. Well, sir?

BROWNLOW. Bedwin, you get blinder every day.

BEDWIN. At my time of life, people's eyes don't improve, sir.

BROWNLOW. Well, well, put on your glasses and see if you can find out why you were called.

OLIVER. Don't you know me, Bedwin?

BEDWIN. God bless my soul! It's Master Oliver come back again! *(She embraces him and holds him out to look at him.)* I knew you'd come back some day. I knew it. *(She looks triumphantly at GRIMWIG.)* And how well you look, too. Color in your face, and dressed like a young gentleman, too. *(She hugs him again.)*

OLIVER. I'm glad to see you, Bedwin. I always meant to come back, you know. And I still remember your muffins.

MRS. MAYLIE. Yes, he compares ours quite unfavorably.

(BEDWIN curtseys.)

BROWNLOW. Now Bedwin, take the ladies and gentlemen upstairs and show them where to lay their wraps, and then serve dinner.

MRS. MAYLIE. But Mr. Brownlow, we're not staying to dinner.

BROWNLOW. That you are, ma'am, and for the night, too. There are a great many things to be talked over here, and I'll not let one of you out of my sight till they are settled.

MRS. MAYLIE. But my dear sir, I've never slept in a strange man's house in my life.

BROWNLOW.   Then it's high time you did, and my sheets are just as well-aired as your own.

HARRY.   *(Offers his arm to MRS. MAYLIE.)* Come, mother. *(As they cross the room.)* We'll stay to dinner anyway. Later we can go to a hotel, if you like.

> *(They follow BEDWIN out. ROSE starts to follow them, but OLIVER stops her.)*

OLIVER.   Please ask her to stay, Rose. I don't want to leave yet.

ROSE.   I will. Besides, there's something I want to know too.

> *(He kisses her hand and she exits.)*

GRIMWIG.   *(Crossing to fire, takes toddy and sits.)* Well, you haven't been idle. Kissing the ladies' hands.

OLIVER.   I'd like to marry Rose, but. Mr. Harry is already grown-up, so I suppose he'll marry her first.

BROWNLOW.   Young men don't marry their sisters.

OLIVER.   But Rose is adopted. And she says she will never marry Mr. Harry until she finds out her own name.

> *(Belt rings.)*

GRIMWIG.   Another orphan the Lord's provided for.

BROWNLOW.   Are you happy with them, Oliver?

OLIVER.   Oh, yes sir, but—

BROWNLOW.   But what?

OLIVTR.   But I'd rather be here with you, sir. You know how it is. A man likes to be with other men.

BROWNLOW.   And so you shall be, Oliver. And I think I have news for you.

GRIMWIG.   Better not count your chickens before they are hatched.

OLIVER.   Are you raising chickens, Mr. Brownlow?

BROWNLOW.   No. Mr. Grimwig is an old nuisance, but the news can wait until the others come in again.

BEDWIN.   *(At door.)* There's a young woman at the door to see Miss Rose.

BROWNLOW.   Oliver, tell Miss Rose someone wants to see her. *(Oliver goes off.)* Well, well, bring her in. Don't stand there looking like that. *(She doesn't move.)* Well?

BEDWIN. I don't like her looks, and she wouldn't give her name. Said Miss Rose wouldn't know her.

BROWNLOW. I'll talk to her.

BEDWIN. And there's a man and a women in the kitchen to see you, sir.

BROWNLOW. Is this house so small that we ask guests to wait in the kitchen?

BEDWIN. Guests, humph! I wouldn't call them guests, and the kitchen is the only place I'd set them too. It's clean, and that's more than they are. And they said you was expecting them, too. Seems to me we're having strange visitors for a respectable house, Mr. Brownlow.

BROWNLOW. That will do, Bedwin. I will see them later. Now show the young woman in.

(*BEDWIN goes up to the door.*)

BEDWIN. You can come in here.

(*NANCY enters, as BEDWIN draws aside her dress, for her to pass the door. NANCY gives her a sullen look, and then looks at the men.*)

BROWNLOW. Now young woman, who is it you want to see here?

NANCY. I want to see Miss Rose.

BROWNLOW. Come now, take yourself off. Miss Rose can't see you.

NANCY. I've been trying to see her ever since she came to London. I followed her here today, and I'll be carried out before I go. (*GRIMWIG rises, looking equal to the task.*) And I'll make such a job of it, that the two of you can't put me out, either!

BROWNLOW. You certainly have brass. How dare you come into my house like this. Bedwin, show her the door.

BEDWIN. You come with me.

NANCY. You heard me. I won't go until I've seen her.

(*ROSE and OLIVER enter.*)

ROSE. You wanted to see me?

NANCY. Yes, Miss—

OLIVER. Nancy!

(*He runs to her and tries to embrace her.*)

NANCY. Don't, Master Oliver. They wouldn't understand it here.

GRIMWIG. I see the connection now, Mr. Brownlow. She is one of the thieves.

ROSE. So you are Nancy, and you gave Oliver the sausages, and threw the whip into the fire when they —

(HARRY enters.)

NANCY. You told her. You peached on us.

OLIVER. I had to tell Rose, Nancy. She's an orphan like us. She understands.

ROSE. You needn't be afraid, Nancy. You can trust us. We are all friends of Oliver's, and we'll be a friend to you, too. *(GRIMWIG grunts.)* Sit down, Nancy.

NANCY. No, it's getting late, and I must go in a minute. *(Nods toward BEDWIN.)* Send her away. I want to tell you something, but I can't talk with that long-faced thing in here.

BROWNLOW. You may go, Bedwin.

(BEDWIN goes, muttering indignantly.)

NANCY. *(Nods toward center door.)* Is that door shut?

BROWNLOW. Yes. Why?

NANCY. I don't want anyone to hear what I'm going to tell you. I'm putting my life in your hands tonight. Oliver can tell you what it means for me if they find out.

OLIVER. Don't do it, Nancy. Don't peach on them. They can't, hurt me now.

NANCY. There's something I must tell you and her. *(Nods toward the men)* Are you sure I can trust them, Miss?

ROSE. I give you my word that nothing you say in this room tonight will ever be repeated. And nothing will ever be used against you.

NANCY. Do you know a man named Monks?

ROSE. Monks? No.

NANCY. Well, he knows you.

OLIVER. I remember him. He came to see old Fagin once.

NANCY. He made a bargain with Fagin that day, to make a thief of you, Oliver. And he came again after you and Bill went to Chertsey, and brought some people with him—those Bumbles you talked about. And they sold him a locket and a ring which they said belonged to your mother.

OLIVER.   They always said that old Mrs. Thingummy left something.

NANCY.   And when they were gone, Monks said to Fagin—"The only proof of the boy's identity will lie at the bottom of the river tonight, and the old hag who nursed his mother is in her coffin." And he said—"I've got his money sewed up now, and thief though you are, Fagin, you've never laid such snares as I'll contrive for my brother Oliver."

OLIVER.   His brother? Oh no, no, Nancy. Not that man's—not Monk's!

BROWNLOW.   Young woman, do you realize what you've said?

NANCY.   Those were his very words, sir. *(Turns to ROSE.)* And he said something about you, too. He said it was the devil's own luck, if the boy fell into the hands of old Maylie and that girl Rose; and that you'd give a thousand pounds to know who the brat really is. And when old Fagin asked him if he knew you, he said he'd had his eyes on you for years.

HARRY.   What?

ROSE.   Harry, who can he be?

HARRY.   Maybe he goes by some other name among us.

NANCY.   Monks is all we know. And I must go now before they miss me.

HARRY.   Wait a minute. Miss Rose has given you her word that we will never repeat what you have told us, but you must tell us more. Tell us where to find this man Monks, and let us deal with him.

NANCY.   I'll not do it. Devil though he is. I'll not betray him.

HARRY.   Why not?

NANCY.   Because we're all in it, and I'll never turn on them.

OLIVER.   Nancy is right. She can't peach on them.

HARRY.   I give you my word that we will not betray the others.

NANCY.   But if Monks turned on them. If he—

HARRY.   If he tells the truth about Oliver, the matter will rest there.

NANCY.   And if not?

HARRY.   The others will not be brought to justice without your consent. Will that do?

NANCY.   If the young lady promises for you.

ROSE.   I do promise, Nancy. All we want is to find out about Oliver.

NANCY.   I've been a liar, and I've lived among liars ever since I was a child, but I'll take your word, Miss. Monks is tall, and has a lurking walk. And constantly looks over his shoulder, first one side and then the other. Remember that, for you can tell him that way. And on his throat, so high that you can see it above his neckerchief —

BROWNLOW.   A bright red mark, like a burn or scald?

NANCY.   You know him then?

BROWNLOW.   I think I do. I've been to the West Indies and back looking for that man. Two days ago, I met him in the street, but he got away. Where does he live?

NANCY.   None of us know that. But there's an inn called the Three Cripples. If you watch for him, I think you can find him there.

(She starts for the door.)

HARRY.   You've given us valuable assistance, Nancy. *(Takes out his money purse.)* Now you must let us do something for you.

NANCY.   There's nothing you can do for me.

ROSE.   We'll look after you, Nancy. You can't go back there now.

NANCY.   It's where I belong.

ROSE.   But we can't let you go like this.

NANCY.   When ladies are young and beautiful like you, they can do as they please. But you're not like me.

ROSE.   Oliver, you speak to her.

OLIVER.   Please, Nancy. Mr. Harry will take care of you, too.

NANCY.   No, Oliver. It's too late for me. If you'd stayed a little longer, you'd know. But you got away in time.

ROSE.   At least let us give you some money. Please, Nancy.

NANCY.   No, I didn't do it for money. I want that to remember. But I would like something that belonged to you…your gloves, or your handkerchief, maybe. *(ROSE gives her a handkerchief. She looks at it.)* Thank you, lady. Good bye, Oliver.

OLIVER. *(Holding her.)* Oh Nancy, stay here with us. We'll never let old Fagin or Bill hurt you any more.

NANCY. No, Oliver, I'm a thief like the rest of 'em, and I'll take my chances with them. Let me go now.

OLIVER. But Nancy, won't I ever see you again?

NANCY. Maybe. Who knows. But best forget all about me now.

OLIVER. Oh Nancy, I'll never forget you—never.

(She pulls away from him and opens door.)

NANCY. Good night. God bless you, lady.

(NANCY exits.)

BROWNLOW. Well, no matter how bad she's been, she's atoned for it tonight.

ROSE. Do you really think she took her life in her hands by coming here?

BROWNLOW. If they ever find out, they'll have no mercy on her. *(GRIMWIG blows his nose.)* Mr. Grimwig, I never heard you keep still so long.

GRIMWIG. There are times, Mr. Brownlow, when even I have nothing to say.

BEDWIN. *(Entering.)* There are some men at the door asking to see you, sir. They said to tell you they have your man.

BROWNLOW. *(Rushing out.)* They got him! They got him!

MRS. MAYLIE. *(Entering.)* Now what is happening in this extraordinary house?

HARRY. Mother, I think you and Rose had better go upstairs. *(To OLIVER, who starts off after BROWNLOW.)* No, Oliver. Stay here by me.

MRS. MAYLIE. Is something unpleasant going to happen, Harry?

HARRY. I'm afraid so, Mother.

MRS. MAYLIE. *(Taking armchair.)* Then I shall stay.

HARRY. But Mother, there may be trouble.

MRS. MAYLIE. There was trouble long before you were born, Harry, and I find it rather stimulating. *(To ROSE.)* Come here, dear. You look worried.

(ROSE sits beside her. HARRY and OLIVER stand near them.)

A MAN'S VOICE. *(Outside.)* If you're willing to take the chance. Mr. Brownlow—

BROWNLOW. *(Outside.)* He knows the alternative. I'll call if I need you. *(He comes in, speaking to someone over his shoulder.)* Come in here.

MONKS. *(At the door.)* How dare you do this to me?

BROWNLOW. Come in, I say.

MONKS. *(As he enters.)* By what authority am I kidnapped in the streets—and brought here?

BROWNLOW. By mine. You may appeal to the law if you like, but if you do, you'll take the consequences. Better do what I ask. It will be easier here than in a court of justice.

MONKS. Is there no other way?

BROWNLOW. No.

MONKS. This is pretty treatment from my father's oldest friend.

BROWTNLOW. Because I was your father's friend, I am giving you this chance. If you did not bear the name of Leeford, I would send you to prison, where you belong.

MONKS. What do you want with me?

BROWNLOW. You have a brother.

MONKS. I have no brother. I was an only child. You know that.

BROWNLOW. But you have a half brother. And you know that.

MONKS. It is necessary to discuss this before all these people?

(He glances around, and starts when he sees OLIVER.)

BROWNLOW. Yes, I see you do know him. Now will you tell the truth?

MONKS. I have nothing to say.

BROWNLOW. Then the law must take its course. *(Opening the door.)* You are free to go now, but I warn you that the moment you leave here, you will be arrested.

MONKS. What do you want to know?

BROWNLOW. After your father and mother were separated, your father met a young lady by the name of Agnes Fleming. He painted her portrait before he went to Rome. *(He indicates the picture over the fire.)* The girl in that picture is the mother of your half-brother, Oliver.

OLIVER. She is my mother?

BROWNLOW. You, too, see the resemblance. Now I want proof.

MONKS. Why come to me? I have no proof.

BROWNLOW. You did have them.

MONKS. How do you know that?

BROWNLOW. By your own words to the head of that thieves' den. "The only proofs of the boy's identity will lie at the bottom of the river tonight."

MONKS. Who told you that? Not Fagin.

BROWNLOW. No. But every word that passed between you and Fagin is known to us.

MONKS. If you know it all, what more do you want?

BROWNLOW. I want justice for Oliver. Your father made a will leaving half of his fortune to you and your mother. The other half to Agnes Fleming and her child. What happened to that will?

MONKS. My mother burned it, as any woman of spirit would have done. She never forgave my father for leaving her. After he died, we tried to find the Fleming girl, but she had disappeared. Later, we learned that she died.

BROWNLOW. Mr. Grimwig, will you ask the people in the kitchen to come here. *(GRIMWIG does.)* Then it was not until you saw Oliver at old Fagin's, that you realized you had a brother?

MONKS. We heard there was a boy, and something he said about being born in a Workhouse made me suspicious.

MRS. MAYLIE. If you are one of those thieves, perhaps you can tell me something about the robbery in my house, last winter.

MONKS. Housebreaking is not in my line, Mrs. Maylie.

OLIVER. *(Crosses to Monks.)* Are you really my brother?

MONKS. Yes, worse luck. I wish you'd died with your mother. Then I would have been free of the lot of you.

OLIVER. Why did you bargain with Fagin to make me a thief?

MONKS. According to my father's will, you forfeited your share if you did anything that was criminal before you came of age. And my mother made me promise that if you ever crossed my path, I would hunt you down and make you suffer. I'd have done it too, if somebody hadn't blabbed.

GRIMWIG. *(Enters with the BUMBLES.)* Here are your kitchen guests. Mr. Brownlow.

BUMBLE. *(Sees OLIVER.)* Do my eyes deceive me, or is that little Oliver? Oliver, don't you know me? *(Starts forward with hand extended, but MRS. BUMBLE pulls him back.)* If you only knew how we grieved for you.

MRS. BUMBLE. Hold your tongue, Bumble.

BUMBLE. Can't I have feelings when I see Oliver here among ladies and gentlemen?

GRIMWIG. You'd better restrain your feelings.

BUMBLE. And I loved him as me own. Master Oliver, you'll remember how I used —

OLIVER. I remember how you used to beat me.

BROWNLOW. *(Motioning to Monks.)* Do you know this man?

BUMBLE. *(A look from MRS. BUMBLE stops his greeting.)* N—n—no.

BROWNLOW. *(To Mrs. Bumble.)* Perhaps you do, Mrs. Bumble.

MRS. BUMBLE. I never saw him in my life.

BROWNLOW. Or sold him anything, perhaps?

MRS. BUMBLE. What do you mean? No.

BROWNLOW. Then where is the locket and ring that belonged to Agnes Fleming?

MRS. BUMBLE. I don't know what you're talking about.

BROWNLOW. Perhaps this pawnbroker's ticket will remind you?

MRS. BUMBLE. Well, if he's coward enough to confess, I have nothing more to say. I did sell them to him, but they are where you'll never find them again *(To MONKS.)* You sneak! *(To BROWNLOW.)* What else do you want?

BROWNLOW. Nothing, but I shall see to it that you are never in a position of trust again. *(To BUMBLE.)* Nor you either.

BUMBLE. It was all Mrs. Bumble. I was the one to tell her it would get us in trouble, sir.

GRIMWIG. That's no excuse for you. In the eyes of the law, a man's wife acts under his direction.

BUMBLE. Then the law is a bachelor, and speaks without experience.

MRS. BUMBLE. Do you mean we lose our places in the Workhouse?

BROWNLOW. That is exactly what I mean. You will never mistreat children there again. You may go now. *(To MONKS, as he starts out.)* No, not you.

GRIMWIG. Come on. Get out of here.

MRS. BUMBLE. *(As they go.)* Next time, I'll leave you at home.

(They are gone.)

MONKS. What more do you want of me?

BROWNLOW. Will you sign a confession, giving us in detail what you have told us here?

MONKS. Yes.

BROWNLOW. And turn over to Oliver half of your father's estate?

MONKS. There isn't much left. Six thousand pounds, perhaps.

BROWNLOW. Then three thousand must come to him.

HARRY. And now do you know this young lady?

MONKS. Yes.

ROSE. I don't know you.

MONKS. I've been watching you for years.

HARRY. You must explain that.

MONKS. Oh, must I?

HARRY. You'll never leave this room until you do.

MONKS. High-handed, aren't you? *(To ROSE.)* Agnes Fleming had a sister, and when she and her father died, the little girl was adopted by—*(looking at MRS. MAYLIE)*—a rich lady.

MRS. MAYLIE. Well, sir, what was the lady's name?

MONKS. I guess you know that, Mrs. Maylie.

ROSE. Do you mean that —

MRS. MAYLIE. Rose, my dear!

MONKS. The girl in that picture is your sister.

BROWNLOW. And Oliver is your nephew.

MRS. MAYLIE. But you are none the less my daughter, Rose, and always will be. *(To MONKS.)* If you have known it for years, why didn't you tell us before?

MONKS. I never wished any of her family any good. *(To BROWNLOW.)* Where's your confession? I want to get out of here.

BROWNLOW. Mr. Grimwig, will you come with me to witness this man's signature?

GRIMWIG. I will, but he's so tricky, that even then I'll not be sure it is his.

   (They go out.)

MRS. MAYLIE. I think we'd better go to our rooms. I've found this a bit more stimulating than I bargained for. Good night, Oliver.

HARRY. But Mother, we haven't had dinner yet.

MRS. MAYLIE. I'll have my dinner in bed. I haven't the moral courage to face that man Grimwig any longer. *(To OLIVER.)* You are a good boy, Oliver, and I am fond of you. Come, Rose.

ROSE. I'll come in a moment. *(HARRY takes his mother out. Looking at the picture.)* I can't believe it yet.

OLIVER. I'm glad I belong to you Rose. I like having a relative.

ROSE. I can just remember her a little. Seeing the picture brings it back. When we go home tomorrow, I'll try to tell you something about her.

OLIVER. But Rose, I—I promised Mr. Brownlow I'd stay here.

ROSE. Oh Oliver, not now! Just when I've found you!

OLIVER. I'm sorry. But he found me first. I wish I'd been twins, then one of me could stay with you too. But you don't mind. You still have Mr. Harry.

ROSE. But Harry doesn't really belong to me.

OLIVER. He'd like to, and it's foolish to keep him waiting any longer, now that you have a name. And a relative.

ROSE. Oliver, who told you that—

OLIVER. I can see. Your eyes shine whenever he comes into the room, and you always sing more when he is at home, too. *(As HARRY re-enters.)* Mr. Harry, I want to ask you a question—man to man.

ROSE. Oliver!

OLIVER. Now Rose, you keep still. This is man to man, I said. Do you love Rose?

HARRY. Yes, Oliver, I do. But she knows that.

OLIVER. And are your intentions honorable? Do you mean to marry her?

HARRY. *(Gravely.)* I do.

OLIVER. *(Takes Rose's hand.)* Then as her one living male relative, I give you my consent. *(Puts ROSE'S hand in HARRY'S.)* She is yours to have and to hold until death do you part.

HARRY. Thank you, Oliver. Where did you get that about death do you part?

OLIVER. Rose read it in a story. Wasn't that right?

HARRY. Quite right, Oliver, if Rose agrees with us. Do you, Rose?

ROSE. Yes, Harry.

BEDWIN. *(Entering.)* Beg pardon, Miss, but your aunt wants you to come to her at once. She can't get into any of my nightgowns, and she don't know what to do about it.

ROSE. I must go to her, Harry.

HARRY. We'll both go, Rose.

(He puts his arm around her, and they go out. BEDWIN stares after them in horrified.)

OLIVER. It's all right, Bedwin. He's going to marry her.

BEDWIN. *(Delighted.)* I knew it, the minute I laid eyes on them. You'll be growing up before long, Master Oliver, and getting married, too. What are you doing with that snuffbox?

OLIVER. Mr. Brownlow uses it, and so does Mr. Grimwig.

BEDWIN. Yes, they've settled all their arguments with snuff for years, but that don't recommend it to me. And that man Grimwig— *(Bell rings off.)* That'll be the nightgowns again. But as I was saying, that man —

OLIVER. You'd better go, Bedwin. Mrs. Maylie likes people to be prompt.

BEDWIN. Oh, she does, does she? Well, she can just wait until I get there. As I was saying, that man Grimwig—

(GRIMWIG and BROWNLOW appear at the center door. BEDWIN shuts her mouth suddenly, and goes out.)

BROWNLOW. Well, I call that a good day's work.

GRIMWIG. Who told you about Leeford's last will?

BROWNLOW.   I didn't know there was one. That was a shot in the dark. And it hit. Well, Oliver?

OLIVER.   Now that you've found me again, what are you planning to do with me?

BROWNLOW.   First, I'm going to educate you. There will be three thousand pounds from your father's estate. And I'll adopt you, and make you my heir.

GRIMWIG.   Humph!

BROWNLOW.   And what have you to say against that, Mr. Grimwig?

GRIMWIG.   Nothing, Mr. Brownlow. What would be the use?

BROWNLOW.   There's a becoming spirit of humility in you at last, Mr. Grimwig.

GRIMWIG.   Humility the devil! You are a stubborn old fool, and you would do just as you pleased, regardless of what I said.

BROWNLOW.   I hope you will always remember, Mr. Grimwig, that I said Oliver would come back.

GRIMWIG.   He didn't come back. He was brought back.

BROWNLOW.   Mr. Grimwig!

(He reaches for his snuffbox.)

OLIVER.   Here it is, sir.

(They take snuff, and shake hands as the lights fade.)

END

Other Titles Available from **Classic Youth Plays**

HIAWATHA
By James Norris

Native-American history comes to life in this true and exciting story of how Hiawatha made peace among the Iroquois and formed the first League of Nations. The play includes colorful dances and ancient rituals making this a truly remarkable theatrical experience.

LINCOLN'S SECRET MESSENGER
By Charlotte B. Chorpenning

All of the intrigue and drama of the espionage plots which characterized Washington DC during the Civil War play out in this historic drama. Chorpenning's detail of authenticity includes using actual dialogue from speeches of people in the plot to assassinate Lincoln making this a remarkable drama for young audiences

ROBINSON CRUSOE
by Madge Miller

Based on the story by Daniel Defoe, this humorous adaptation brings new life to the tale of the shipwrecked Crusoe. Written by the acclaimed playwright, this highly theatrical version of the tale is entertaining and cleverly crafted. Suitable for touring.

TITIAN
by Nora Tully

The Italian Renaissance is reconstructed in this story of the boyhood of the famous painter Tiziano Vecelli, later called Titian. This realistic play for youth is a moving portrait of the young artist and the struggles he had to overcome to achieve his goals.

YOUNG JOAN OF ARC
by Emma Gelders Sterne

A powerful and moving play. The story of Joan of Arc presented from the viewpoint of her family and neighbors. Told with lyrical realism, the play focuses on the girlhood of the The Maid of Orléans as she comes to terms with her destiny.

For a complete list of Classic Youth Plays from Theatre Arts Press visit

ClassicYouthPlays.com

Printed in Great Britain
by Amazon

13189434R00041